Driving the Back Roads

The Amish
In the World, but Not of It

by
Reynold R. Kremer

Kremer Publications, Inc.
Butler, Wisconsin

All Scripture quotations, unless otherwise indicated, are taken from the HOLY BIBLE, NEW INTERNATIONAL VERSION®. Copyright © 1973, 1978, 1984 by International Bible Society. Used by permission of Zondervan Publishing House. All rights reserved.

The "NIV" and "New International Version" trademarks are registered in the United States Patent and Trademark Office by International Bible Society. Use of either trademark requires permission of International Bible Society.

All rights reserved. No part of this publication may be reproduced, stored in a retrieval system, or transmitted in any form or by any means–electronic, mechanical, photocopying, recording, or otherwise–except for brief quotations in reviews, without prior permission of the author.

Kremer Publications, Inc.
12615 W. Custer Avenue, Butler, WI 53007
www.kremerpublications.com
© 2006 Reynold R. Kremer
Published 2006
Printed in the United States of America
ISBN 0-9745631-5-3

Cover photos by Reynold R. Kremer
Cover design by Julie A. Barthel

To my wife Edith,
who knows and lives the
true meaning of Christian partnership.
Without her this book
would never have been possible.

TABLE OF CONTENTS

Foreword

Chapter 1:   **The "Radical Reformers@**   9
The Reformation Climate and Martin Luther
The Swiss Reformation
Anabaptism Is Born
The Martyrs

Chapter 2:   **Anabaptist Foundations**   24
A Change of Life
The Schleitheim Articles
The Dordrecht Confession of Faith
Methods of Evangelism

Chapter 3:   **A Home for the Hutterites**   42
A Fascinating History
The Hutterite Life
Hutterite Worship
The Dining Hall
Hutterite Education
Hutterite Farming and Commerce
Hutterite Women
Courtship and Marriage
The Hutterite Family
Sports and Leisure
Hutterite Dress
Hutterites Today

Chapter 4:   **Menno Simons Takes Over**   64
Mayhem at Münster
Menno Simons Takes Control
William Penn=s AHoly Experiment@
A Dangerous Journey
The Mennonites Today
Old Order Mennonites
Moderate Mennonites
Main Body of the Mennonite Church
The German Baptist Brethren

Chapter 5:   **Amish Riddles**   80
Jacob Ammann Disagrees
Gelassenheit
The Ordnung
No Telephone
No Cars
No Electricity

Chapter 6:   **The Amish at Worship**   95
The Church District
The Worship Service

The Singing
The Communion Service and Foot Washing
Choosing Bishops, Ministers, and Deacons
Amish Divisions
Old Order Amish
New Order Amish
Beachy Amish
Amish Mennonites

Chapter 7: Within the Amish Community — 110
Birth
Education
Rumspringa
Courtship and Dating
Baptism
Weddings
The Grandpa House

Chapter 8: Amish Traditions — 127
Dress
   Children's Clothes
   Women's Wardrobe
   Clothing for Men
Sewing and Quilting
Diet
Barn Raisings
Language
Amish Names
The Horse and Buggy

Chapter 9: An Amish Day — 144
A Day of Honest Housework
Farming and Lunch-pail Work
Recreation and Relaxation
Health
Folk Medicine
Hospital Treatment
Hereditary Diseases
Mental Illness
Funerals
Tourism

Chapter 10: Personal Reflections — 164
It Seems So Good
All Is Not as It Seems
Problems with the Government
Too Difficult to Discuss
Never Certain of Salvation
God Is a Gracious God
Intimidation and Fear
God Is a Loving God
Sharing with the Amish

Bibliography — 180

PREFACE

Amish is a religion! The Amish clock did not simply stop ticking. Amish is a religion. The Amish people are not museum employees trying to show outsiders how things were done 100 years ago, nor are they entertainers like those who put on Civil War reenactments. Amish is a religion. Many tourists love to sneak photos of these unique people who seem so vulnerable and helpless. They are neither. They are a religion. The Amish do what they do for one reason only: it's their religion. And they are not ashamed to let the world know that they are different. They are proud to be a people "in the world, but not of it."

This is the study of a religion that began at the front door of a church in Wittenberg, Germany, where a young man named Luther nailed Ninety-five Theses. Lutherans, Reformed and Anabaptists grew out of that movement. We are about to focus especially on the Anabaptists and their descendants, the Hutterites, Mennonites and the Amish.

Many people enjoy the friendly shops, craft stores, restaurants and overall homey feeling they get when they visit Shipshewana, Indiana, or Lancaster County, Pennsylvania. These are fun and interesting places where millions of tourists walk the streets and sidewalks to contribute to the million dollar industry spawned by these Plain People. Few however take the time to learn much about them. Instead they just shrug their shoulders and admit that the sights are great, the products are well-made, but none of it makes any sense.

In this book we will find some answers to the whys and wherefores of these people. It is indeed a difficult puzzle to piece together, but if we look at the puzzle pieces one by one, we begin to see what it is that makes this culture exist as it does.

Throughout this book I have attempted to treat these people with utmost Christian respect. The Plain People deserve neither ridicule nor stoning, nor even odd looks. Instead we must begin to understand them in order to see their ways and their faith. Only then can we respond.

I would like to give special thanks to author Ruth Irene Garrett, for the valuable time she spent with me. Thanks to Ruth and her husband Ottie, I was able to ask the tough questions that only a former Amish person could answer. Ruth left her Amish home in Iowa to marry an "English" man. As a result she was excommunicated (by her bishop uncle), and shunned. Since then she has become a contributing member of Mt. Hope Lutheran Church (LCMS) in Bowling Green, Kentucky. Her candid answers to a multitude of questions gave me insights that no books could have. To Ruth and her husband I am most indebted.

I would also like to offer special thanks to Pastor Reuben Kleinsasser and the people of the Springfield Hutterite Colony just outside Winnipeg, Canada, for the hospitable tour, dinner and personal "concert" they gave my wife Edith and me, and to Hutterite Pastor Edward (last name withheld) for kindly answering my questions and reviewing the chapter on the Hutterites. Thanks are also in order for John and Esther (last name withheld), an Amish couple in Indiana, who took time to show us their home-based business and graciously invited us into their home, and to Mennonite pastor Joseph Yoder, head curator of the Menno-hof Museum in Shipshewana, Indiana, for sitting down with me and answering my many questions. Very special thanks also go to best-selling author Beverly Lewis who gave of her time to clarify a number of important points.

Now let's jump into the car and head toward the back roads. Just maybe we'll see one of those buggies clippety-clopping along the shoulder, or maybe we'll happen to see an Amish woman hanging out her wash, or just maybe we'll catch a glimpse of some Amish kids running barefoot on their way to school.

Reynold R. Kremer

CHAPTER 1
The "Radical Reformers"

If you ever traveled the back roads of Wisconsin, Illinois, Indiana, Ohio or Lancaster County Pennsylvania, you probably caught a glimpse of an intriguing world. Many tourists enjoy a leisurely drive through "Amish country" in hopes of sneaking a photo or two as they pass a horse and buggy, a schoolyard filled with barefooted children, aproned women hanging their laundry on the washline, or bearded men straining in the fields with their horse-drawn plows. Some travelers even take the time to stop at a local Amish grocery store to stock up on bags of dry soup mixes and snacks, or at a local Amish furniture shop where they marvel at the hand rubbed dining room tables and chairs. They may even hope to see the artistry of the $1500 handmade Amish quilts that would certainly beautify any bed.

It takes little time to realize that this is a unique group of people who value hard work, appreciate the simpler things in life, and aren't ashamed to look different from the rest of the world. After all, this is not your "normal" 21st century western culture. It's almost like looking through a giant picture window into a living and breathing museum. And what makes the view even more intriguing is that all the people in this museum are alike. The men all wear beards and large rimmed black hats. The women walk around with their long dark dresses. The young ladies all cover their heads with white, starched bonnets, and the lads wear their un-parted hair cut exactly to ear length.

The more you see, the more you can't help but ask the same questions that everyone asks. When did the clock stop? Why would anyone want to live this way? What would cause an entire society to resort to this radical way of life? Where did this old-fashioned culture begin, and how long can it possibly go on?

Finding answers to these questions is like putting together the pieces of a giant jigsaw puzzle. There certainly are questions–lots of them! But there are answers too. If we carefully study the puzzle pieces and place them together in the correct order, we will begin to see the complete picture of the Amish culture, a culture that is in the world, but not of it. It's a fascinating journey that begins over 450 years ago, halfway around the world, with one simple incident–a baptism!

The Reformation Climate and Martin Luther

Martin Luther was born in 1483. Although the year may not be significant of itself, the era certainly was. The Middle Ages were nearing an end, and the civilized world was waking from a thousand year sleep. Little did anyone realize that it was about to encounter a reformation that would shake its very foundations. For us today, it's hard to imagine the impact that Luther made that October 31 in 1517, when he stepped up to the Wittenberg church door and posted the Ninety-five Theses.

That moment sparked both a religious and social reform that would change the face of Europe. God's wheels of Sola Fide (by faith alone), Sola Scriptura (by Scripture alone), and Sola Gracia (by grace alone), were beginning to turn. For years the people of Europe had lived under the dark cloud of the papacy and the Holy Roman Empire. These two powerful forces had joined hands in a religious-political siege that kept the masses in check for centuries. They ruled with an iron fist over Europe's social, religious, and economic culture. They dictated what was and what was not to be preached. They controlled the status of the people. They held the strings of the money bags that were filled with coins from taxes and indulgences. They were answerable to none, and they guaranteed that anyone who questioned their authority would be quickly silenced.

But the winds of reform didn't begin with Martin Luther. They started to blow many years before Luther was born. As early as 1176, Peter Waldo, a merchant from Lyon, France, attempted to lead people back to the Scriptures. He taught the people that the Bible was to be read, loved, and believed. His followers, the Waldensians, sold their property and devoted their lives entirely to God, a conviction that cost many their lives.

John Wycliff was another reformer in the 1300's. He took to the highways preaching that the Word of God should be accessible to everyone. This "Morning Star of the Reformation" began his career as a professor at Oxford University. He ended it as one of the great reformers of the church. His outspoken hatred for the sins of the clergy and papacy, and for the offensive sale of indulgences (documents sold to the people in return for a shortened term in purgatory) set him at such odds with the Catholic Church that after he died and was buried, his bones were exhumed, burned, and tossed into a river along with his books and other writings.

Following closely behind Waldo and Wyclif was John Hus. Also a university professor, Hus was outspoken in exposing the evils of the papacy and the immorality of the church. Hus was invited to a general council of the church in Constance in 1415. Although he was promised safe passage, at his arrival he was arrested, put on trial, and sentenced to death. From within the prison cell John Hus wrote, "It is better to die well than to live well. One should not flinch before the sentence of death. To finish the present life in grace is to go away from pain and misery."[1] Martin Luther knew the great sacrifice made by John Hus when he remarked, "In John Hus the Holy Ghost was very powerful."[2]

Driving the Back Roads

People in sixteenth century Europe continued searching for an escape from the political, social, and religious tyranny and control. Consequently many misguided people began to follow radical leaders. Some of these charlatans spent their time playing with toys and babbling like babies claiming that Jesus commanded them to become as little children in order to enter the kingdom of heaven. Others, like the Adamites, convinced their followers to run naked through the woods. The Free-livers boasted having several wives in common, and the Weeping Brothers held highly emotional prayer meetings.[3]

By the mid 1500's God decided the time was right to place a flamboyant Catholic professor named Luther at the entrance to the church of Wittenberg. Luther was about to make a bold stand before the nobles and the church hierarchy. Europe and the world would never be the same. On October 31, 1517, Martin Luther posted his proclamation of ninety-five statements regarding the sale of indulgences. He demanded a debate. He believed the church had overstepped its bounds and had miserably lost sight of the true light of God's grace. Luther respected the church, and wanted to see it return to the teachings of the apostles. He never wanted to destroy the church, but rather to open its eyes and to refocus its sight on the only path to heaven as found in the pages of Scripture. Little did Luther realize that on that crisp October day he was actually drawing a line that would one day divide the Roman Catholic Church from an increasing number of protesters.

From England to the Alps, from the Netherlands to Austria people discussed the growing climate of reform. Luther's arguments with the Catholic Church were welcomed and appreciated by many throughout Europe. Even the smallest burgs and hamlets buzzed with interest. At long last the people had a glimmer of hope to help them escape the church and state domination. Not coincidently, shortly before this time God opened the mind of a brilliant inventor named Johann Gutenberg to discover the use of movable type. That single invention made it possible to print great numbers of books and pamphlets in a short amount of time. Printed media made Luther's Reformation the topic of the day. But Luther wasn't the only one engaged in reforming.

The Swiss Reformation

Ulrich Zwingli was born in 1484, two months after Martin Luther. He shared more with Martin Luther, however, than just a similar birthday. He too wanted to reform the church. Zurich, Switzerland was the stage for his reformation. A former Catholic priest, Zwingli, like Luther, preached against the depravity of the Catholic Church, claiming that indulgences, the mass, and monasticism were not scriptural. He is credited with founding the Swiss Reformed Church.

Zwingli was an avid reader of Luther's writings and was greatly influenced by his German counterpart. In 1518 he was appointed head pastor in the city of Zurich, where his popularity gained him support of the city council. This acceptance was significant because church practice, doctrine, and worship were all controlled by the council, not the local church. In those days it was not unusual to hear the local officials discuss church business such as preachers, worship, and church building programs. After all, that was how a state church was conducted.

Zwingli's reformation would not have succeeded without the blessing of the local council. He knew he needed their support. What he didn't realize, was that at the same time he was succeeding with his reformation, another reformation was growing within the walls of his very own church.

Besides the churches begun by Luther, there was another child born to the reformation. This child claimed to be neither Reformed nor Lutheran. Its members were dissidents that arose from Ulrich Zwingli's own congregation. They were the Anabaptists, a group of "radical reformers" who traveled a different path in their reformation. Today in the United States we see the offspring of the Anabaptist movement in the churches known as the Mennonites, the Hutterites, and the Amish.

Anabaptism Is Born

The history of the Anabaptists is a sad journey that winds through the valleys and mountains of Europe where the Mennonites, Hutterites, and Amish were forced to make many painful trips in search of a homeland. Over the years these three Anabaptist groups headed in different directions, explaining why they share common roots of deep Anabaptist conviction and belief, yet they practice lifestyles that are quite different from each other. The ultra-conservative ways of the Old Order Mennonites, the Hutterites, and the Amish seem to defy reason and common sense. Many view their way of life as a riddle. Yet the riddle can be answered by looking into their detailed history books.

> **CONRAD GREBEL**
> **1489-1526**
> The son of a wealthy nobleman, Grebel studied in Vienna, Paris, and Zurich, and became a proofreader for Latin books. Grebel was at first a close acquaintance of Zwingli but later the two were at odds because of the issue of infant baptism. Grebel died of the plague at age thirty-seven.

The vibrant and intellectual nature of Ulrich Zwingli's church often attracted gifted young scholars. In the early 1520's a handful of young men began to meet regularly for study of the Greek classics, including the Greek New Testament. Within a short time, the discussions began to center around various aspects of the church, especially the reformation. There were three men in particular who shared this interest, Felix Manz, Conrad Grebel, and George Blaurock. These young men made it known that they disagreed with the direction in which Luther's

> **FELIX MANZ**
> **1498-1527**
> A native of Zurich, Mantz was a brilliant scholar in Latin, Hebrew and Greek. He often served as the "reader" at the meetings. Manz was drowned at age twenty-nine in the River Limmat that flows through the city of Zurich.

reformation was headed. They felt Luther did little to encourage a change in the lifestyles of the people. Manz, Grebel and Blaurock believed that only those who applied the command to follow Christ and lived lives of self-sacrifice and deprivation could be truly considered Christian. They claimed it was necessary to sever all ties, not only with the established church but with the state as well, in order to be completely free and independent to live their lives in devotion to God. Accordingly, their hope was to create a society that would no longer be controlled by the church or by the state. Luther's reformation, they maintained, was only a partial reformation. Whereas Luther's energies were directed toward reform within the church, Manz, Grebel and Blaurock felt Luther stopped short of severing all ties with the state. "Luther", wrote the *Hutterian Chronicle*, "broke the pope's pitcher but kept the pieces in his hands. Luther and Zwingli acted like two men trying to mend an old kettle, while only making a bigger hole."[4]

Although the Anabaptists often paired Luther and Zwingli together because of their "lack" of social action, Martin Luther and Ulrich Zwingli actually parted ways with one another over the doctrines of the Lord's Supper and Baptism. Zwingli professed the Reformed view that the Lord's Supper merely represents the body and blood of Jesus and serves as only a reminder of Christ's suffering and death. Luther on the other hand held to the words of Scripture in which Christ says, "This 'is' my body and this 'is' my blood." The earthly elements neither represent (Reformed doctrine) nor become (Catholic doctrine) the body and blood of Christ. Rather Scripture maintains that body and bread, blood and wine, are all present in the Lord's Supper. Zwingli, who relied heavily on human reason, also doubted the validity of infant baptism. Moreover, Zwingli and Luther disagreed on the roles of the church and state. Whereas Luther felt the state was to provide peace so the church could function, Zwingli felt the state was there to be used by the church to accomplish its purposes.

The Bible meetings in Zwingli's church, initiated by Grebel, Manz, and Blaurock, continued into the middle 1520's. They discussed many topics at these meetings, but infant baptism always seemed to demand the most attention. Both the Catholics and Lutherans agreed that Scripture declares that the Old Adam is passed down from generation to generation beginning with Adam and Eve. From the moment of conception the sinful nature is present in us, and therefore infants are indeed sinful and need to be washed clean from their sins and be adopted into God's family. This washing is done through the Sacrament of Holy Baptism. But the three maintained the view that nowhere in Scripture is infant baptism specifically commanded by God, and if it is not commanded, it should not be done. Instead, they said, baptism should be reserved only for those who are mature enough to make a heartfelt pledge to daily take up their cross and follow in the footsteps of Jesus Christ. This way they could be assured of a pure church made up of true believers. They called it "believer's baptism." Conrad Grebel makes this point in a letter written to Thomas Muntzer on September 5, 1524:

> GEORGE BLAUROCK
> 1492-1529
> Blaurock was a student of the Catholic Church, beginning as a monk and eventually a Catholic priest. A strong leader in the early Anabaptist movement, and highly regarded by the Mennonites., Blaurock was burned at the stake in the region of the Tyrol in 1529.

> "We hold that all children who have not attained the knowledge to discern between good and evil and have not yet eaten of the tree of knowledge are surely saved through the suffering of Christ...In answer to the charge that faith is required of all who are to be saved, we exclude children and...that they will be saved without faith and that they do not believe...Infant baptism is a senseless, blasphemous

abomination contrary to all Scripture." (Edited by Leland Harder, 1985.)[5]

Zwingli became increasingly concerned with the growing popularity of these three young men and soon severed ties with them, siding with the city officials. (At first Zwingli agreed with the radicals not to baptize infants, but later he changed his mind.) In August, 1524, the Zurich Council issued a proclamation that only infant baptism was tolerated and anyone who withheld a child from the Sacrament of Baptism would be fined and punished. Furthermore, they demanded that the Bible study meetings led by these three men were to be disbanded. The city council asked Zwingli to meet with "The Swiss Brethren" (*Schweizerische Bruder*), as they now began to call themselves, with the hope of changing their minds. Several meetings were held in January of 1525, but they failed to resolve their disputes–especially regarding the question of infant baptism. The Swiss Brethren held fast to their conviction that baptism should be reserved for adults who could promise a lifelong commitment to the Lord.

January 21, 1525, was a historic night. Anabaptists maintain this was the date that their church was founded. The *Hutterian Chronicle* describes what took place that evening in the house of Felix Manz:

"When the reformers were meeting, fear came upon them and they fell to their knees and prayed with all their hearts to the almighty God of heaven. They asked God to have mercy on them for what they were about to do. They were well aware that this could lead to suffering and punishment. After the prayer ended, George Blaurock stood and asked Conrad Grebel to baptize him. As he said this, he knelt down and was baptized by Grebel since there was no pastor in the room. Then the others present asked Grebel in turn to baptize them as well. And so, in the fear of God, these men surrendered themselves to the Lord. Some present were commissioned to teach and to spread the gospel message. This was the beginning of separation from the world and its evil ways."[6]

At first glance it might seem that this small band of religious "radicals" secretly baptizing one another was hardly significant. That couldn't be further from the truth! This was sixteenth century Europe. By this single act these men defiantly severed all ties with both the established Roman Catholic Church and the emerging Protestant reformers by their reinvention of baptism. But that was not all. This baptism carried with it significant political importance as well. Not only were they declaring a basic church teaching invalid, but it was through baptism that a child's name was placed on the public roles for them to be eventually taxed and enlisted into the military. Abolishing infant baptism put a swift end to this practice. January 21, 1525, laid the foundation of a wall that would separate the Swiss Brethren from the Roman Catholic Church, the young Lutheran Church, the Reformed Protestant churches, and the city of Zurich. In essence these men claimed that no one maintained any more control over their public or private lives. They declared themselves free to think, believe, worship, and do as they wished. A church could no longer dictate beliefs, and a state could no longer control their actions. Is it any wonder that before long both the church and the state aimed their wrath at this small group of upstarts who were trying to create their own Radical Reformation with its own form of "heresy"?

Soon the Swiss Brethren were given the distasteful title of "*Wiedertäufer*" ("rebaptisers"), or the name still used today, "Anabaptists" ("*ana*" is Greek for "again"). State and church leaders attempted to bring a swift end to this newly formed church. They were not about to be upstaged by a band of young radicals and their handful of misguided followers. Within four months the first Anabaptist was arrested, tried, and sentenced to death.

Public records show that two years after the Zurich meeting, twenty-nine year old Felix Manz was arrested, sentenced, and drowned in a Zurich river. George Blaurock was burned at the stake in 1529. However instead of putting out the flames of this movement, the persecutions caused the radical reformation to spread faster than could be imagined. Disciples were fleeing for refuge throughout Europe. Germany, Moravia, and the Netherlands became the scenes of many secret Anabaptist meetings and worship services. This geographical movement would later result in the three major divisions of Anabaptism–the Hutterites, the Mennonites, and the Amish. Church and civil authorities took drastic measures to destroy this "menace". It was about time for one of history's bloodiest persecutions.

The Martyrs

The *Martyrs Mirror* is a collection of accounts and court records of those who died in the great persecution. (The proper title is *The Bloody Theater or Martyr's Mirror of the Defenseless Christians*.) Compiled in the mid 1600's by a Dutch Mennonite minister, its object was to remind future Anabaptists of the carnage and terror experienced by the early Anabaptists. This already huge volume was amended in the later 1600's when Mennonite artist Jan Luyken added 104 copper engraved illustrations. The 1100 pages of the *Martyrs Mirror* are stained with the blood of more than 600 martyrs from the Netherlands and nearly 200 more from other parts of Europe, all executed for their unwavering beliefs in the Anabaptist teachings. Even today this book is found in most Amish homes and Anabaptist ministers still frequently refer to it in their sermons. Page after page of the *Martyr's Mirror* tells the story of pacifist martyrs who were tortured by dismemberment and branding, and killed by fire and drowning. The carnage was rampant throughout

Europe–from Salzburg to Augsburg, from Brussels to Cologne, from Venice to Amsterdam. Here's how the *Martyr's Mirror* reads: (From the 25th edition by Herald Press, 2004.)

JACOB DE MELSELAER, A.D. 1558

In the year 1558, Jacob de Melselaer, a brother, was apprehended at Antwerp, for living according to and keeping the Word of God; who, after much examination and torment, as he would not renounce or apostasize, was condemned to death, and brought forth into the marketplace, with a gag in his mouth, to prevent him from speaking. Nevertheless, he went to death with boldness, and valiantly testified with his blood to the faith he confessed.

FRANS TIBAN AND LITTLE DIRK, A.D. 1558

Two brethren named Frans Tiban and Little Dirk, were apprehended for their faith at Antwerp, examined, tortured, afflicted with much torment, and, finally, as they would in no wise apostasize, condemned to death, and beheaded in prison.

GRIETGEN, TANNEKEN, LIJNTGEN, AND STIJNTGEN OF AIX-LA-CHAPELLE, A.D. 1558

Four sisters, named Grietgen, Tanneken, Lijntgen and Stijntgen of Aix-le-Chapelle were apprehended at Antwerp, on account of their faith, and severely examined; but as they could in no wise be moved therefrom, and fought as heroines for the name of Christ, always firmly adhering to the truth, they were finally tied crooked and drowned in prison.[7]

Although numbers are somewhat vague, it is estimated that between 1525 and 1580 nearly 4000 Anabaptists lost their lives because of their faith. Even the *Ausbund*, the hymnbook still used today in Old Order churches, contains fifty-three hymns penned by imprisoned Anabaptists.

Another account is of Gerritt Hazenpoet, a young tailor who lived in the Netherlands. Gerrit was arrested when he tried to secretly return home to visit with his wife and children. Prior to his execution the authorities held a mock banquet, a common occurrence. Court records list the costs connected with his execution:
1. Police to capture him
2. Executioner to torture him
3. Rope for torture
4. Wine for the executioner and local lords
5. 24 days worth of food for the prisoner
6. Supply of fuel, straw and hay
7. Court proceeding
8. Payment to a doctor and church prior who attempted to get him to recant
9. An executioner to kill him
   Total spent: 37 guilders ($70 today)[8]

Again we read in the *Martyr's Mirror*:
"Some were racked until the sun could have shown through them, so that some were torn and died, some were burned to ashes under the name of heretic, some roasted on pillars, some torn with glowing tongs, some locked in houses and all burned together, some hanged to trees, but some executed with the sword, killed and cut to pieces. Many were gagged or had their tongues tied so that they should be unable to speak or defend themselves, and were thus led to their death...Like lambs they were led to the slaughter in droves and murdered according to Satan's kind and nature."[9]

But Anabaptism was far from being destroyed. The flames that consumed the innocent martyrs only ignited the faith and perseverance of the survivors. Those who silently died for their beliefs went proudly to their graves believing they had presented their Lord with the ultimate sacrifice.

In their quest to find a peaceable homeland, one small band of believers headed in the direction of Austria–the future Hutterites. Another group still sought freedom in the Netherlands–the Mennonites. A third band moved into Switzerland and France and would eventually break away from the Mennonite community–the Amish.

1. Cornelius J. Dyck, *An Introduction to Mennonite History*, p. 26.
2. L. Fuerbringer, *The Concordia Cyclopedia*, p. 341.
3. John A. Hostetler, *Amish Society*, p. 26.
4. www.anabaptistchurch.org/chronicle2.htm.
5. Edited by Leland Harder, www.anabaptistnetwork.com.
6. www.anabaptistchurch.org.
7. Excerpts taken from *Martyrs Mirror*.
8. John S. Hoyer, *Mirror of the Martyrs*, p. 21.
9. www.mhsc.ca/encyclopedia/contents/M37857.html.

CHAPTER 2
Anabaptist Foundations

To solve the puzzle of the Plain People we must also understand their religion, for it is their belief system that lies at the root of their Old Order way of life. (The Plain People here refers to the Hutterites, Old Order Mennonites, and Old Order Amish.) Let us not forget that their church began during a period of tremendous religious, political, and social unrest. Religion and government were both in serious confusion. Anabaptism was but one of the reforms that came about. Their leaders were staunch Christians who knew their Bibles well and were willing to die for their convictions. They did not arrive at their teachings haphazardly. Much study and debate went into the formulating of their doctrine, and even they did not agree with one another on every point. Although we realize that their belief of baptism was at the heart of their faith, we also take a close look at the rest of their beliefs to get the entire picture.

Therefore, to understand the ways of the people who live on the back roads, we must look deeply into their religious convictions and teachings.

A Change of Life

Anabaptists call Luther's reformation incomplete. Why? Luther attempted to bring the church back into the pages of Scripture, because that is where he found the true meaning of God's grace and mercy. He rediscovered the truth that salvation is based entirely on the justification that was won by the blood of Jesus Christ, to which the believer then responds with a life of sanctification. God's child reacts to God's love by living a life that reflects that love. Scripture plainly declares that "We love because he first loved us" (1 John 4:19).

The "Radical Reformers" felt that Luther's emphasis on faith fell short of the mark. While they agreed there was a need for faith, they placed an added emphasis on the outward life of the individual. They objected to the followers of Luther and Zwingli who appeared to make no changes in their way of living. "They resisted the 'salvation by faith only' theology of Luther. They were convinced that 'grace' as understood by Luther resulted in a license to sin."[1] While faith was important, living a life of true sacrificial Christianity was necessary first. This is clearly seen in all early Anabaptist writings and it is lived out today in the lives of the Old Order Mennonites, the Hutterites, and the Amish who practice extreme sacrifice, humility, submissiveness and obedience, and design church rules and regulations demanding that this standard of life be carried out in every detail.

The Schleitheim Articles

Anabaptists are quick to point out that their religion is not based on "man-made" creeds or articles of faith. Their fear is that outward statements threaten the supremacy of Scripture. Consequently, although the writings of several early Anabaptist leaders still exist today, little has been written to organize their beliefs. This is one

> **MICHAEL SATTLER**
> **ca. 1490-1527**
> Michael Sattler was very influential in the movement of the Swiss Brethren. Born and raised in the area of the Black Forest in Germany, Michael was a prior in a Benedictine monastery until about 1526 when he joined forces with the Anabaptists. He was involved in secret conferences in Schleitheim where he was instrumental in writing the Schleitheim Articles. Following the Conference he was arrested and put on trial.

reason why there is such a variation in the branches of Anabaptism. However, there are two confessions that the Anabaptists point to as statements of their faith.

The first confession is called the Schleitheim Articles. Written in 1527, the intent of these articles was not to be a formal declaration of faith, but rather to present arguments against the established church. These articles, written by Michael Sattler of Stauffel, Germany, sum up seven major doctrines of Anabaptist faith that set them apart from the state churches of their day.

Article One: Baptism

Baptism should be reserved only for those who consciously realize that their sins have been forgiven and who can promise a conscious walk as a believer. This excludes baptism of infants–which is stated as the "chief abomination of the pope". (The Anabaptists believe that children are immune from God's wrath because their wrongdoings are not counted against them.)

Of all the areas of disagreement with the Catholic and Lutheran teachings, this was the greatest, and remains so today. The Anabaptists are insistent in their belief that only adults who promise to sacrifice everything and turn their lives over to the Lord are worthy to be baptized. First faith, then baptism. The more conservative Anabaptists practice their "believer's baptism" as they call it, between the ages of eighteen and twenty-four. The Anabaptists also define baptism differently. Whereas Martin Luther wrote that "baptism works forgiveness of sins, delivers from death and the devil and gives eternal salvation to all who believe," the Anabaptists claim that baptism is instead a vow to remain faithful to Christ and to live a life of submission to his teachings.

Article Two: The Ban (Excommunication)
After one has been baptized and enters the community of believers, he or she must remain true to God and the community. If they falter, following the dictation of Matthew 18, they will be banished from communion.

The Anabaptists follow the words of Matthew 18 which set in place an orderly system to deal with those who are in need of repentance and absolution. The Anabaptist practice of excommunication is intended as a gesture of love to show the sinner his evil ways and to bring about a repentant heart. This article proved to be instrumental in leading to the formation of the Amish sect. As will be seen later in the Dordrecht Confession, the Amish believed the ban was also to include the practice of shunning.

The Anapabtists placed great importance on the term "community of believers". Today this can be seen in the closed societies of the Amish and Hutterites. To these groups the "community" of the church is a very important part of their existence. Perhaps because of the loose membership of the established church of the Middle Ages, the Anabaptists believed that the church was to be a living entity that established standards for the entire community. "The underlying assumption was simple: the collective wisdom of the church superceded the freedom and rights of the individual."[2] As will be seen, the Amish today strictly follow the unwritten rules and ordinances established in each individual church community.

Article Three: Breaking of Bread
The Lord's Supper is given to remember the suffering and death of Jesus Christ. Only those who are of the community of Christ may partake of the Lord's Supper.

The Canadian Conference of Mennonite Brethren Churches defines the Lord's Supper as: "Pointing to Christ, whose body was broken for us and whose blood was shed to assure salvation for believers and to establish the new covenant. In the Supper the church identifies with the life of Christ given for the redemption of humanity and proclaims the Lord's death until He comes. The supper expresses the fellowship and unity of all believers with Christ. It is a supper of remembrance, celebration and praise which strengthens believers for true discipleship and service."[3] The Anabaptists view the Lord's Supper much like the Reformed. Martin Luther was deeply at odds with the Anabaptists for their teaching of representation. Since the Anabaptists did not believe that Christ instituted the sacraments, they placed little importance on the Sacrament of Holy Communion, as can be seen in Jacob Ammann's proposal to increase the offering of the Lord's Supper from once to twice a year.

> **Article Four: Separatism**
> All members will remain separate from the sinful world. They will have no fellowship with the world. Instead they will live their lives as a separate community by themselves. This includes no taking up of arms for protection.

Anabaptists adhere strictly to the command of 1 John 2:15: "Do not love the world or anything in the world. If anyone loves the world, the love of the Father is not in him." One Anabaptist remarked that they separate themselves from the world because that is an "alien environment with thoroughly different ethics and goals."[4] Today this can be seen especially in the ways of the Amish, Hutterites, and Old Order Mennonites, who shape a society that avoids contact with the outside world. (The Amish call the non-Amish "English".) They note that the world hated

Jesus (John 15:18: "If the world hates you, keep in mind that it hated me first.") and the whole world lies in wickedness (1 John 5:19: "We know that we are children of God, and that the whole world is under the control of the evil one.") Their avoidance of all contact with the outside world takes on a very ironic twist today, especially in areas like Lancaster County, Pennsylvania. This huge Amish settlement is one of the most heavily trafficked tourist areas in the country. Here live a people who want nothing more than to be left alone, but instead they are hounded by tour buses, cameras and thousands of sightseers.

With Christ as their model, the Anabaptists also consider themselves conscientious objectors. Many European wars were fought between professing Christians, which to the Anabaptists appeared to be a strange contradiction. How could Christians claim to love one another, said the Anabaptists, when they wage war against their own kind? Michael Sattler wrote, "If warring were right, I would rather take the field against so-called Christians who persecute, capture, and kill pious Christians than against the Turks...The Turk is a true Turk, knows nothing of the Christian faith, and is a Turk after the flesh. But you who would be Christians and who make your boast of Christ persecute the pious witnesses of Christ and are Turks after the spirit!"[5] The objection to taking up arms has caused great suffering in nearly every country where these people have sought a home, always putting them at odds with their government. Yet the Anabaptists cling fervently to Christ's command to turn the other cheek. Menno Simons wrote, "All Christians are commanded to love their enemies; to do good to those who abuse and persecute them...Tell me, how can a Christian by Scriptures defend retaliation, rebellion, war, striking, slaying, torturing, stealing, robbing and plundering and burning cities, and conquering armies?"[6] Today this issue has been carefully dealt with by the United States and Canadian governments. Now many young Anabaptists serve time at voluntary service centers.

The strict adherence to no service in the military varies widely among the various branches of Anabaptism, from swift excommunication for joining the military to simply preaching against the evils of war. It should be noted, however, that many Anabaptist organizations have donated tremendous amounts of money to world disaster relief, disability programs, foster care, and other social causes.[7]

This article also says it is wrong for the Anabaptist to take someone to court. One will not find an Anabaptist named in a lawsuit except in extreme situations. They would rather suffer the harm brought upon them than take another person to court. In recent times this has led to the dilemma of outsiders taking advantage of them, especially in business matters, realizing they are safe from retribution of lawsuits.

Article Five: Pastors in the Church

Upon baptism, all male members are eligible to be called full time to serve as the congregation's pastor. This lifelong calling includes the roles of teaching, preaching, admonishing and leading in prayer.

Along with a young man's baptism vow is his promise to serve as minister if ever called upon. This he will do gladly and willingly, although he will never make a conscious effort to attain such a calling. Unlike many established churches today, the Anabaptists (especially the Amish and Hutterites) have no seminary or formal place for training their religious leaders. They believe it is a sin to flaunt one's ego or even to study more deeply than necessary the truths of Scripture. Therefore further education is strictly forbidden. In most cases the pastors have the same eighth grade training as the rest of the males in the community. When a Hutterite pastor was asked about his professional training, he waved his arm pointing to all the buildings of his colony and said, "Here is where I get my training". The lifelong calling has at times been the cause of great frustration in some church communities, with little hope of replacing a pastor who does not serve his congregation well.

Article Six: The Sword of the Government
The role of the government is to keep in line those outside of Christ's church. No one shall serve in government office, vote or serve in the military.

The Anabaptists believe that government was established by God as Paul wrote in Romans 13. They also believe that the role of the government is to wield the sword and to keep mankind in check. However, the Anabaptists also feel that the government was not intended for them. The government is only to rule over those outside the church of God. They are free from government rule since they are under the direct governance of God.

The Amish are forbidden to run for office apart from perhaps a local school board. They cite three reasons for this decision. First, running for office is a sign of personal arrogance and ego, not to be a part of true Christian humility. Second, it means they participate in serving the sinful, worldly state. Third, an elected official may need to enter litigation as a state representative, which would go against their beliefs.[8]

Yet there are instances when the Plain People must bow to the wishes of the government. Even the Amish today must pay taxes and obey civil laws. (They do not, however, pay Social Security Tax because they refuse to collect it.) For instance, the Amish must display the safety triangle on the back of their carriages and use directional signals. Amish dairy farms must also submit to strict milk cooling procedures and other regulations to be allowed to sell their milk to the public.

Article Seven: Oaths
Christ forbids all swearing, for that is used to settle any quarrels and for making promises. Only yea or nay are necessary. Anything more is evil.

The Anabaptist believes that those who live in the Truth speak the truth. Therefore there is no need for oaths. They claim that Christ himself forbade us from swearing oaths. Perhaps this view began in the sixteenth century when oath taking was a very important part of showing allegiance to the state. It is even recorded that many European cities set aside a special day each year called the "Day of the Oath" when citizens would have the opportunity to stand in front of the local churches and swear their faithfulness to the state.[9]

The Dordrecht Confession of Faith

In 1632, sensing a possible rift within the church, a group of Dutch Mennonites addressed eighteen points of doctrine. Their purpose was to write a simple confession that clarified certain Anabaptist teachings, especially avoidance or shunning of excommunicated members. The Dordrecht Confession of Faith was accepted by many of the Anabaptist congregations. In 1725, when a group of Dutch Mennonite pastors met in southern Pennsylvania to establish their roots here in the new world, it was the Dordrecht Confession of Faith, not the Schleitheim Articles that they chose as their doctrinal standard. The Amish today consider this their chief confession.

The eighteen points of the Dordrecht Confession: (Paraphrased from a translation by J. C. Wegner in *Introduction to Theology*, Copyright 1954.)[10]

1. Regarding God and the Creation
God is the maker and preserver of all things and he created the world in six days. When God finished his

creating work, he formed Adam of the dust of the ground, and breathed the breath of life into his nostrils so that he became a living soul in God's own image. Afterwards he took a rib from Adam and made the woman, giving her to him for a helpmeet, companion and wife.

2. Regarding the Fall into Sin
Adam and Eve were deceived by the serpent and sinned against God's command. Sin at that moment came into the world, and this sin is now passed upon all men, for all have sinned, and they were sent from Paradise to till the earth and eat the bread produced from their sweat. Through this one sin they became estranged from God and were eternally lost, had not God in his compassion, stepped in with his love and mercy.

3. Regarding the Promise of Christ
God was not willing to cast off man because of his sin, or to let them be forever lost, but he called them to him and comforted them giving them a hope that there was still a way to become reconciled to God, namely through the Lamb, the Son of God who would redeem and raise up fallen man from his sin, guilt and unrighteousness.

4. Regarding Christ in This World
When the time had come, God sent this promised Messiah, Redeemer, and Savior into the world, even in the flesh. He was conceived of the virgin Mary, who was engaged to a man named Joseph, of the house of David. She gave birth to him in Bethlehem, wrapped him in swaddling clothes and laid him in a manger.

5. Regarding the New Testament
Before his ascension, Christ instituted his New Testament and gave it to his disciples and sent them into the world to preach the Gospel message.

6. Regarding Repentance
Since the imagination of man's heart is evil from his youth and prone to sin, the first lesson of the New Testament is repentance and reformation of one's life, that those who hear God's Word must reform their lives, believe the Gospel, put out the old man, put on the new man, and forsake sin. For not even Baptism or the Lord's Supper can, without faith, change or renew life. We must go to God with an upright heart and in perfect faith, and believe in Jesus Christ that we might be forgiven, sanctified and justified, and made children of God.

7. Regarding Holy Baptism
We confess that penitent believers, who through faith are made one with God, must, upon their confession of faith, and renewing of life, be baptized with water in the name of the Father and of the Son and of the Holy Ghost, according to the command of Jesus Christ. His sins will thus be buried and he will be brought into the communion of saints.

8. Regarding the Church
Those who truly repent, believe, and are baptized comprise the visible church of God. These are the chosen generation, the royal priesthood and the holy nation, declared to be the bride of Christ and children and heirs of eternal life. This church shall withstand floods and tempests, even the gates of hell.

9. Regarding Church Leaders
Before Christ's departure, he left his church equipped with faithful ministers, apostles, evangelists, pastors and teachers, who, with the help of the Holy Ghost, govern the church, feed his flock and watch over and protect his church. These are to be an example, light and pattern, worthily administering the baptism and the Lord's Supper and providing for all the needs of the church. Furthermore, deacons and deaconesses were appointed to visit and care for those in need.

10. Regarding the Lord's Supper
We observe the breaking of bread, or Supper, as that which the Lord Christ gave to his apostles before his death. We observe it in remembrance of Christ, who commanded that it should be observed in the remembrance of his suffering and death. This he did out of his great love toward us sinful men. This meal admonishes us to live up to the unity and fellowship which is in God and is signified by the breaking of bread.

11. Regarding the Washing of the Saints' Feet
We confess a washing of feet for our fellow saints because Jesus instituted and commanded it when he washed the apostles' feet, thereby giving us an example to wash one another's feet as a sign of true humility and to remember that by this washing we are likewise washed through his precious blood. (Foot washing is still practiced today in some Anabaptist circles who believe that Jesus instituted foot washing in John 13:14,15, as a sign of cleansing both body and soul. Many churches

use this practice especially prior to worship services that celebrate the Lord's Supper.)

12. Regarding Marriage

We believe in the honorable state of matrimony, of two free, believing persons, in accordance with the manner God ordained it in Eden. We believe that just as the patriarchs had to marry among their kindred, so the believers in the New Testament have no other option than to marry those who have become united with the church, have been baptized, and stand as one in faith, doctrine and practice.

13. Regarding the Government

God ordained power and authority and sent them to punish evil and protect the good, to govern and maintain countries and cities in good order. We may not despise, revile or resist them, but honor them as ministers of God and be subject and obedient to them. We must faithfully pay custom, taxes and tributes even as Jesus taught us. Prayers must also be offered for them and their welfare and for the prosperity of the country that we may have protection and lead a peaceable life.

14. Regarding Revenge

We believe that the Lord has forbidden all revenge and retaliation and commanded not to repay evil for evil, cursing for cursing, but to put the sword into the sheath. We must not inflict pain, harm, or sorrow upon anyone, but seek the salvation of all men. We must pray for our enemies and feed them when they are hungry and thirsty. Finally, we must do good according to the law of Christ to do unto no one that which we would not have done to us.

15. Regarding the Swearing of Oaths

We should not swear at all for we understand that all oaths are forbidden and instead we must answer with yea and nay in all honesty.

16. Regarding Separation from the Church

When someone sins unto death, either willingly or unwillingly, thereby becoming separated from God and forfeiting the kingdom of God, that such a one, after the deed has been made known in the church, shall and must be separated, put away, reproved before everyone, and purged as leaven. And finally, that the sinner may not be condemned with the world, but become convinced and moved to sorrow, repentance and reformation.

17. Regarding Shunning (*Meidung*)

If anyone, because of his perverted doctrine or wicked life, has fallen so far that he is separated from God, and punished by the church, that person must, according to the doctrine of Christ and the apostles, be shunned by all his fellow members, especially those to whom it is known, in eating, drinking, and other similar intercourse, and no company be had with him, they may not become contaminated nor made partakers of his sin. Yet, in shunning, moderation and discretion must be used that it may lead, not to the destruction but to the reformation of the sinner. We will render assistance if the shunned individual is hungry, thirsty, naked, sick, or in any other distress. We must not count them as enemies, but admonish them as brethren, that they might be brought to the knowledge of repentance and sorrow for their sin, so that they might become reconciled to God, and be received again into the church, and that love may continue with them. (Shunning will be covered in greater detail.)

18. Regarding Resurrection and the Last Judgment
We confess with our mouths and believe with our hearts that according to Scripture, on the last day all men who shall have died, and fallen asleep, shall be awakened and shall rise again through the power of God, and that they shall be changed in the twinkling of an eye, and at the sound of the last trumpet, shall be placed before the judgment seat of Christ. The good shall be separated from the wicked, and everyone shall receive in his own body according to what he has done whether good or evil. The pious shall be taken up with Christ and enter into life eternal, and the wicked shall be cast into outer darkness, even into the everlasting pains of hell, where worm shall not die, nor fire be quenched, and where they, according to Holy Scripture, can expect no hope, comfort, or redemption.

Methods of Evangelism

There is great variation in the amount of church outreach carried on by the various Anabaptist churches. Although all of them assist in social problems like creating homeless shelters or supporting soup kitchens, organized evangelism efforts differ widely, from the near nonexistent Hutterite mission program to the extremely zealous Mennonite effort. The more conservative the group, the less evangelism they carry out.

The Middle Ages was a time of very little outreach in Europe. Since Christianity was the state religion, there appeared to be little need to put any effort into the salvation of lost souls. But this changed with the Anabaptist movement. Suddenly a new faith arose with such vigor and vitality that evangelism once again became important to those in this new church. In the very first year of the movement several dozen missions were begun around Zurich and Bern.[11] As early as 1527, an organized evangelism plan was carried out by the Anabaptists in Bavaria. Although many of the evangelists met with premature death, people saw that this was a church on the move. The term "Martyr's Synod" was often used to describe this movement.[12] It is ironic that the Hutterites, who carry on little or no outreach today, were especially zealous in doing evangelism in those days.

The new church could not long survive the persecution that followed its ambitious mission work and before long this practice came to an abrupt halt. For the next 250 years, Anabaptist evangelism was forced underground. No longer safe for members to declare oneself an Anabaptist, the church became known as "the quiet in the land."

Today the Mennonites share a particular interest in evangelism with missions on all corners of the globe. As early as 1851, the Mennonites began an intense mission program. By the late 1800's, foreign missionaries were sent to Africa, India and Turkey.[13] Today's missions continue that fervor. Some Mennonite estimates claim as many as one million converts world-wide.[14] Their mission programs consolidate the Word of God with community, education, and social assistance. The Mennonite Central Committee, based in Akron, Pennsylvania, boasts an evangelism budget near $70 million with over 900 missionaries in fifty countries.[15]

The Hutterites and Old Order Amish refrain from any organized effort. (There are Amish groups not of the Old Order that do carry on mission programs.) They believe it is far more important to be missionaries by example, letting their actions influence those around them. That is why it is such a great embarrassment to an Old Order Amish community when one of its youth is arrested for drunkenness, or disorderly conduct. The Hutterites, once the most zealous of missionaries, are today far

39

less likely to conduct any evangelism. It is estimated that in the past 100 years there have been less than 50 converts to the Hutterites. Hutterite traditions call for a time of probation for anyone who wishes to join the colony. They do not force their ways on others, and are very careful as to who enters their inner circles. A prominent Hutterite pastor said, "Hutterites as a whole do not practice evangelism or mission outreach. The Schmeideleut group has a few evangelism programs. They have an all black colony in Nigeria where some of their people are there at all times. Groups also travel to Romania to help build houses, farm buildings and orphanages. They also support an orphanage in Haiti."

Evangelism remains a point of contention among the Anabaptists. Author Donald B. Kraybill puts it this way, "There are only two ways for many of these colonies and churches to grow: by making converts or by making babies and raising them to claim the faith for themselves. Groups who lose many of their children and gain few converts, will in time, of course, diminish or even die."[16]

1. Publication Board of the Eastern Pennsylvania Mennonite Church, *The Swiss Anabaptists*, p. 123.
2. Donald B. Kraybill, *Anabaptist World USA*, p. 46.
3. www.mbconf.ca/confession/lordssupper.en.html.
4. http://mbconf.ca/believe/pamphlets/anabaptism.en.html.
5. Walter Klaassen, *Anabaptist: Neither Catholic nor Protestant*, p. 60.
6. William R. Estep, *The Anabaptist Story*, p. 60.
7. Donald B. Kraybill, *Anabaptists World USA*, p. 49.
8. Donald B. Kraybill, *The Riddle of the Amish Culture*, p. 274.
9. William R. Estep, The *Anabaptist Story*, p. 58.
10. http://www.bibleviews.com/Dordrecht.html.
11. J. C. Wenger, *What Mennonites Believe*, p. 56.
12. Merle and Phyllis Good, *20 Most Asked Questions about the Amish*, p. 48.
13. Ibid, p. 49.
14. Donald B. Kraybill, *Who Are the Anabaptists*, p. 39.
15. Donald B. Kraybill, *Anabaptist World USA*, p. 123.
16. Ibid, p. 65.

CHAPTER 3
A Home for the Hutterites

There are three major churches that consider themselves Anabaptist offspring. The Hutterites or Hutterian Brethren was the first organized group. Although it is the smallest of the three churches, the Hutterites provide a very interesting study. The reason we see so few on the back roads of America is because most Hutterites live in Canada. Drive the graveled back roads of Winnipeg, Manitoba, and you will find dozens of Hutterite communities, each going about its daily business in a quiet and unassuming way. When we begin to look closely at their way of life, we find a group of people who believe that every part of their existence, including worship, dress, home life, and fellowship, reflects the teachings of the Holy Scripture. By following their history and their livelihood, we will provide another piece to our Anabaptist puzzle.

A Fascinating History

Sixteenth century Europe witnessed the growth and dispersion of the Anabaptist believers. As happens with most radical reforms, the faster the growth, the more the hatred toward them; the more intense their beliefs, the greater the effort to destroy them. This was very evident with the Radical Reformation. The result was a rapid movement of severely persecuted refugees. What began with a secret baptism in Zurich, Switzerland, spread to Austria, Czechoslovakia,

Germany, Belgium and the Netherlands. Because of this scattering, many individual Anabaptist groups emerged that took on new, different, and sometimes unusual doctrines and practices. One of these groups was the Hutterites. The Hutterites were the first of the three major Swiss Anabaptist branches to develop. Today they maintain the same strength of conviction and unique lifestyle that they did in the sixteenth century. Although they are first cousins with the Amish and Mennonites, the Hutterites disagree with them in many ways. For instance, the Hutterites dress much like the Amish, yet they own the latest farm equipment. The Hutterites share their belief in baptism, separation of church and state, and objection to war, with the Mennonites, yet they still speak and preach in German. The Hutterites spend their days at work in the fields like the Amish, yet they live in barrack-like homes, eat in a common dining room and share everything they own in a strict socialist society. Now considered the oldest and largest surviving communal society in North America, the Hutterites share a history filled with trouble and sorrow.

The early years of the Hutterite church are stained with blood, unrelenting persecution, and turmoil. Few, if any, religious sects have been hunted, accused, tortured and killed as have the Hutterites.

Anabaptism began in Switzerland, yet it didn't take long to spread to Austria and Bavaria, especially to the region of the Tyrol (present day Innsbruck, Austria.). That region soon came under the harsh rule of Austrian

---

HANS HUT
1490-1527
Born the son of a farmer and a bookbinder by trade, Hut served as a sacristan to several knights. He refused baptism for his infant daughter and spent much of his time handing out pamphlets of Martin Luther. In 1526 he was re-baptized as an adult. He is best known for his disputes with Balthasar Hubmaier in Moravia. He escaped for his life but was captured and sentenced to be burned at the stake. History records that he committed suicide before his execution could be completed.

Archduke Ferdinand, who vowed to destroy the Anabaptist "menace". This tyrant went so far as to establish the *Tauferjäger* or "Anabaptist hunters". These were specially chosen men who were commissioned to track down, arrest, and bring their captives to swift trial. Specially appointed judges swiftly handed down the same sentence to all Anabaptists: death. Those who recanted of their radical beliefs, were "mercifully" killed by beheading, instead of the burning, drowning and dismemberment reserved for the more stubborn brothers and sisters. It wasn't long before several Anabaptist families headed east and north of the Danube River into the region of Moravia. This area was still considered a relatively safe place for the reformers. Many families settled in and around the town of Nikolsburg, Moravia (present day Mikulov, Czechoslovakia.). The migration was so successful that by 1527 there were an estimated 12,000 Anabaptists living in the region. Such a rapid influx of strangers alarmed the local citizens, who were rapidly becoming outnumbered. They hoped to put a halt to any new arrivals, but were soon stopped by the local noble, himself an Anabaptist convert, who suggested instead that the Anabaptists be allowed to move into the region if they agreed to help defend the territory from outside attacks by the Turks. Although this arrangement seemed a fair resolution to the problem, it was soon met with mixed reactions by the Anabaptists.

Balthasar Hubmaier, a former acquaintance of Ulrich Zwingli, enjoyed the peace he found in Nikolsburg and sided with the noble by agreeing to pay a war tax. Hans Hut, another Anabaptist leader, vehemently disagreed. Hut believed that the Turks were carrying out God's wishes by destroying the evil rulers of Europe. He and his followers flatly refused to pay any tax that would be used for military purposes. This and other pressing issues, such as the date of Christ's return and visions and dreams were debated by Hut and Hubmaier at the Nikolsburg Disputation held in May, 1527. Hans Hut was soon seen as one who defied the civil authorities with seemingly little concern for the Anabaptists' safety in Moravia. Hut's views met with such disdain that he was imprisoned in Nikolsburg Castle. Some say that one of Hut's followers, concerned for Hut's life, rescued him late one night by lowering him through a window in a rabbit's snare net. Although Hut fled, he left behind a sizable group of followers. A wedge was being driven through the Moravian Anabaptist community, dividing the followers of Hubmaier (the *Schwertlers*, "bearers of the sword"), and those of Hans Hut (the *Stablers*, "bearers of the shepherd's staff".)

Balthasar Hubmaier was less fortunate than Hut. He was taken back to Austria and questioned for his Anabaptist beliefs and then sentenced to die by fire. On March 10, 1528, Hubmeier was led to the stake. Gunpowder was rubbed in his hair and beard to hasten his death. Some claim that he shouted, "O, salt me well. O, salt me well." Then he raised his head toward heaven and exclaimed, "O dear brethren, pray that God gives me patience in this my suffering. Jesus! Jesus!" As he finished speaking, flames surrounded his body. Hubmeier's wife Elsbeth stood by giving him encouragement in his suffering. Three days later she was arrested, sentenced, and drowned in the Danube River.[1]

With the passing of Hubmaier, the Schwertlers soon disbanded. However such was not the case with Hut's Stablers. In the spring of 1528, the small congregation of 200 was forced to leave its home in Nikolsburg. As they reached the outskirts

---

BALTHASAR HUBMAIER
1481-1528

Balthasar Hubmaier was born in Bavaria. He attended the University of Freiburg and graduated with a Masters degree in 1511. He served as a devout Catholic pastor until he met Ulrich Zwingli in 1523. That relationship began to fail as a rift arose over infant baptism. More and more Hubmeier believed along the Anabaptist lines of personal sacrifice and adult baptism. He fled to Moravia where his preaching is credited to the conversion of thousands to the Anabaptist faith. In 1527 he and his wife were arrested and taken to Vienna, Austria, where he was tried for heresy, convicted and burned at the stake.

of the city their leaders gathered them together. There they spread their cloaks on the ground and encouraged everyone to place all their material possessions on them, promising to share everything with one another just as the early Christians did in Acts 2:42-44 and 4:32 where "they devoted themselves to the apostles' teaching and to the fellowship, to the breaking of bread and to prayer...All the believers were together and had everything in common...All the believers were one in heart and mind. No one claimed that any of his possessions was his own, but they shared everything they had." Those with great wealth shared equally with those who had little or nothing at all. This practice of communal sharing has since been the identifying mark of the Hutterites. Under the theme of love the Hutterites still hold true to the conviction that anyone who will not give up all worldly possessions cannot be a true follower of Jesus Christ.

The small band of believers finally found refuge in the nearby Moravian town of Austerlitz. Throughout 1528, the group faithfully practiced their belief of sharing, yet they had great difficulty agreeing on the leadership roles within their growing church. In 1529 Tyrolian Pastor Jakob Hutter visited Austerlitz and was immediately impressed with the church's attitude toward communal living. Within a short time Hutter was appointed to head their church. Hutter was a great leader for two years, after which he was forced to flee back to the Tyrol because the Austrian Archduke Ferdinand had renewed his effort to exterminate all Anabaptists. Within a few months Hutter and his wife were arrested, and in February, 1536, Jakob Hutter was publicly burned at the stake. His legacy however, lives on as this small band of Moravian believers took

> **JAKOB HUTTER**
> ? - 1536
> A hatmaker or *Hutter* by trade, Jakob Hutter became an avid Anabaptist living in the Tyrol region. He made a great impact on the Anabaptists who were forced to move from Nikolsburg to Austerlitz, Moravia. Hutter was arrested in Innsbruck in Tyrol where he was later executed. The Hutterites bear his name.

upon themselves the name of *Hutterische Brüder*, the Hutterite Brethren.

The years following Hutter's death were met with optimism as peace reigned throughout the region. The Hutterite church began to flourish. Much of the success was due to the faithfulness of one particular elder named Peter Riedemann. Riedemann was credited with writing The Confession of Faith which the Hutterites still use today as an important doctrinal statement.

The years between 1565 and 1592 became known as the "golden period", because those years allowed the Hutterites to grow to over 100 communes or *Bruderhofs* with an estimated 20,000 to 30,000 members. This time of peace also provided an opportunity for the Hutterites to organize their Bruderhofs into orderly communities of harmony, structure, and purpose. During this time the Hutterites also claim to have begun the first kindergarten and carried out very aggressive mission work. They set as leader of the entire brotherhood a bishop who would regularly visit the colonies. In turn, each individual colony appointed one or more preachers or pastors to serve as their religious directors. Supporting him was a council of leaders who were appointed to oversee the administrative affairs of the colony.

> **PETER RIEDEMANN**
> **1506 – 1556**
> Peter Riedemann was born in Silesia and grew to be a cobbler. In 1529 he was arrested, tortured and after three years released. This scene was duplicated in 1533 when again he was arrested and imprisoned for four more years. A third time he was imprisoned at Marburg where he wrote The Confession of Faith. Riedemann died in Hungary after serving the church for 27 years–nine of which he spent in prison.

But the peace did not last. Between 1600 and 1700 the Hutterites were once again scattered throughout the region by renewed hatred toward their cause. The "Thirty Years War" (1618-1648) was especially hard on pacifists who refused to defend themselves and take up arms. Moravia meanwhile wavered from a Catholic state to Protestant state and back to a Catholic state once again. At the end of the war the Hutterite population had decreased from an estimated 30,000 to a mere 1000. It was however during this period that a great many sermons or *Lehren* and *Vorreden* were recorded and preserved. Many of these sermons are still used today in Hutterite worship services.

Finally, in 1770, a Russian general invited the small remnant of Hutterites to settle in the Russian Ukraine. This band of only 123 believers (including fifty-six former Lutherans), found new hope in the northeast. For nearly 100 years they lived at peace amid the promise that they would not be ordered to take up arms or to pay any more war tax.[2] During this period, three men of distinction, Michael Waldner, Darius Walter and Jacob Wipf, began their work among the Hutterite community. But the Hutterite peace came to yet another abrupt end in 1871 as the Russian government rescinded its promise. They required military service of all available Hutterite males and school attendance of the Hutterite children. Once again, the Hutterites were faced with the problem of searching for a friendly homeland.

> **THE HUTTERITES**
> Total population: 45,000
>
> Dariusleut
>   150 colonies
> Lehrerleut
>   135 colonies
> Schmiedeleut
>   (Oiler & Gibb colonies)
>   185 colonies
> Bruderhof (Arnoldleut)
>   5 congregations

A promising New World lay across the Atlantic Ocean that would provide them the safekeeping and privacy they longed for. From 1874 to 1876, under the continuing leadership of Walter, Wipf, and Waldner, the entire Russian Hutterite community set out on a journey that would take them to the shores of North America. Their eventual goal was to settle in the Dakota Territory where there was unlimited land and the hope of a peaceful way of life. The Hutterites were settled in their new home by 1877.

The communal groups that headed west were divided into three parties: the Schmiedeleut (*Leut* in German means "people". The group was named after their founder Michael Waldner, a blacksmith or *Schmied*) established their first colony called the Bon Homme Colony in 1874 near Yankton, South Dakota; the Dariusleut Hutterites (named after their organizer Darius Walter) established the Wolfcreek Colony near Olivet, South Dakota, in 1875; and the Lehrerleut (named after Jacob Wipf, a popular teacher or *Lehrer*) began in 1877 at the Elm Spring Colony. A fourth group, consisting of nearly half the total number of Hutterites, established individual farms and did not live the communal lifestyle. These were known as the Prairieleuts or non-colony people.

During the next forty years the colonies flourished and grew to almost twice their original size, numbering about seventeen colonies. This was due in part to their large families of between seven and ten children. New land was purchased and a new colony was established whenever a Bruderhof grew to over one hundred members.

Yet once again the peace and calm of their new home was shattered by the cannon blast of war–this time it was World War I. The Hutterites became easy targets as local hatred rose against anyone associated with the German culture. Hutterite speech, pioneer-type clothing, refusal to bear arms, and unwillingness to support the war effort brought new problems and sufferings to their communities. Cattle was stolen and sold for money to finance the war, and their German dialect was forbidden.

A story is told of three brothers, Joseph, David and Michael Hofer, and their close friend Jacob Wipf, who were drafted into the U.S. Army. Upon refusing to serve, they were subject to military discipline and sentenced to thirty-seven years in prison. First sent to Alcatraz, and later moved to Fort Leavenworth, Kansas, these four young prisoners slept on the cold floor in their undergarments because they refused to wear any government issued clothes. Word was eventually sent to their wives that they were ill and near death. When the women arrived they discovered deplorable prison conditions.

Joseph was the first to die. After much insistence to view her departed husband, Joseph's wife was shocked when she discovered his body clothed with full army dress uniform. Her husband was finally forced to wear the uniform he had died trying to avoid. Joseph's brother Michael died a few days later. The other two were eventually released.

This insistence on serving in the military once again prompted the swift movement of the Hutterites as they sought new and safer land. But where could anyone flee to avoid forced military service? Canada was the next stop on the long Hutterite journey. The six Schmiedeleut colonies settled in Manitoba while a handful of Dariusleut and Lehrerleut colonies moved further west into Alberta. At first Canada welcomed the Hutterites to their vast prairies, but before long even they became concerned over their purchase of enormous amounts of land. This concern was soon forgotten as the Great Depression of the 1930's settled in. With both Manitoba and Alberta on the verge of bankruptcy, the Hutterite people were a welcomed friend, able to pay their taxes and care for their own ill and aged members without the need of government assistance. By 1940 there were over fifty colonies scattered throughout Canada.

The 1940's presented yet more problems for the Brethren. Because of their remarkable knowledge of agriculture, they became a threat to other Canadian farmers. New laws were passed. The Hutterites were not allowed to purchase new lands for expansion. No new colony could be established within forty-eight miles of any existing colony, and no colony could exceed 6400 acres. The 1942 Veterans Land Act went so far as to declare that when new land was put up for sale, no Hutterite could bid on it until sixty days had passed. As a result, many

Hutterites again moved back to the states–especially to Washington and Montana.[3]

The Hutterite Life

A visit to a Hutterite colony will give the visitor a true taste of the Hutterite way of communal living. It is estimated that today there are about 45,000 Hutterites living in about 460 colonies in North America. There are about 185 Schmiedeleut colonies in Manitoba, North Dakota, South Dakota, and Minnesota. In 1992 the Schmiedeleut branch divided into two groups because of an argument over liberalism. The less conservative group was called the Oilers (so named because they had money invested in oil) or Group 1. The more conservative branch went by the names of the Gibb Hutterites (named after the lawyer who represented them), the Committee, or Group 2. The 150 Dariusleut colonies are located in the area of Saskatchewan, Alberta, British Colombia, Montana, and Washington. The 135 Lehrerleut colonies reside in Saskatchewan, Alberta, and Montana. The Hutterites have been growing at a rate of about 3% per year.

Each colony is called a Bruderhof or "place where brothers dwell". The communal lifestyle that began in the 1500's is still practiced today. The colony members can be easily recognized on city streets. Their dress, hairstyles, and speech set them apart from the "worldly" crowd. They are a hard working, driven people, who are not ashamed to stand apart from the ways of the world.

There is an elder chosen to oversee several colonies. He is there to help with difficult questions that local ministers may encounter. Ministers are chosen by lot and called upon to conduct the worship services, baptisms, marriages, funerals, and church discipline. Every colony also has a management system consisting of one or two ministers, a secretary, and a farm manager. These meet each morning to discuss daily activities

Driving the Back Roads

and needs. Major decisions are usually discussed at brotherhood meetings of the entire male population. Decisions are voted upon and majority rules.

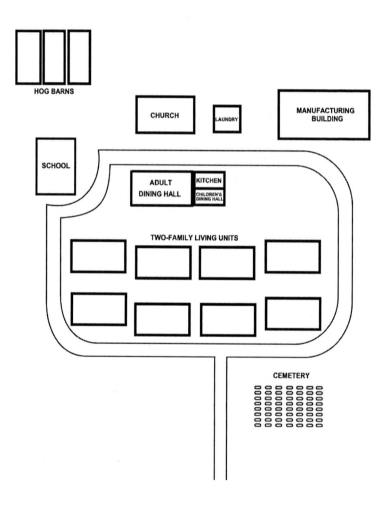

A TYPICAL HUTTERITE COLONY

Colony visitors are not welcomed with open arms. Hutterites are very cautious toward strangers. They do not want outsiders bringing anything into their colonies that might disrupt their way of life. Consequently they follow a set procedure for welcoming visitors into their colonies. Most Hutterite colonies are located well off the major highways, quite isolated from the busyness of city life, and are clearly marked with an attractive sign displaying the name of the colony at the driveway entrance.

Although colonies differ somewhat in their arrangement, most Hutterite colonies follow the same general pattern. As one proceeds down the dirt driveway and nears the buildings, one gets the sense they are about to enter a religious order or college campus because of the organized layout of the colony. One might first pass a well-kept cemetery of simple grave markers for those relatives and fellow members who lived and died in the colony. Entering the colony proper one notices several long barrack-like buildings arranged in a circle or "U" shape. Each building contains two or three duplex apartments for the Hutterite families. Although the "longhouses" look alike, they still take on personalities of their own with chairs, clotheslines, and toys behind most apartments. The Hutterite home is simple with few of the luxuries westerners are used to. They are designed with a living room, a small kitchen, a bathroom, several bedrooms to accommodate their large families (sometimes with nine or more children), and perhaps a sewing room and office. The furniture is plain yet attractive. Shoes are always left at the door before proceeding over the linoleum-covered floors. Unlike Amish homes, it is possible to find some modern amenities in Hutterite homes such as microwaves, sewing machines, or family photos.

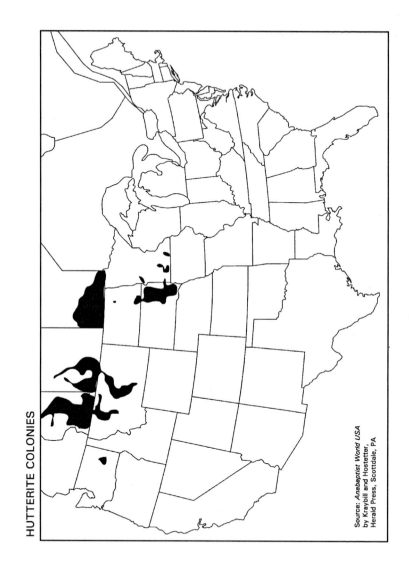

Hutterite Worship

The next buildings one sees will likely be the church, the school building, and the dining hall, each demanding a prominent place in the community.

The church is very plain both in structure and in decoration. There are no stained glass windows, steeple, or fancy doors to welcome worshipers. The inside is filled with pews where the men sit on the left side and the women on the right. Children sit together in the front of the church. Walls are plain, and there is no sign of an altar, chancel, pulpit, or organ. In the front of the church is placed a desk and a chair or two. Since the hymns are sung without accompaniment, one will never hear any instruments in the Hutterite church.

On most days, thirty minute *Gebet* or prayer services are conducted by the pastor before the supper hour. The weekly *Lehr* ("teaching") or Sunday morning teaching service lasts about an hour and a half and includes hymn singing and an hour-long sermon followed by prayer. Hymns are sung in German and are introduced by the pastor who leads by singing the first few lines called "lining". The Hutterites use a hymn book they refer to as the *Lutheran Hymn Book* which contains the German lyrics of several hundred songs. There is no printed music. Thus the pastors must be well versed in leading the congregation in the various hymn melodies. The sermons are usually read by the pastor and may include strong admonitions to the congregation. Pastors often draw the greater portion of the sermon from the *Lehren* or *Vorreden* sermons dating back to the 1500's and 1600's, printed in beautifully bound books. Services are always conducted in German (using a Tyrolean dialect). More liberal groups may conduct the service in English if visitors are present. Luther's German translation of the Bible is the version found in most Hutterite churches. Although many Hutterites today will likely not know Martin Luther, those who are aware of him consider him a brave reformer and are thankful for his translation of the Bible.

Pastors are chosen from within the colony. There is no formal training for them and they serve for life. When it is necessary to choose a new pastor, an advisory board picks several colony members who they think would fit well in that important position. Nominations are made about a week before the actual vote is taken. On the day of the election or *Prediger Wahl*, ministers arrive from surrounding colonies and the vote is cast for one of the candidates. Any candidate who receives five or more votes is eligible to become the next minister. Each chosen candidate then has his name written on a slip of paper that is placed in a hat. The visiting elder draws one name from the hat. That person becomes the next colony minister.[4]

Hutterites celebrate special religious holidays such as Christmas, Easter and Ascension. Special Lehrs may also be held for baptisms and weddings. The Brethren also practice both excommunication and shunning for baptized members who have gone astray. Their reason for the strict procedure is to give the individual an opportunity to see his or her wrongdoings and repent. Following repentance, reconciliation with the colony is gladly offered. Members expelled from the colony are often sent on their way with no money or goods, only the clothes they wear. Some colonies may take up a collection for the departing family.

Hutterite colonies are ruled by the *Gemeinde Ordnung*, the unwritten rules and regulations established by the colony through ministers' conferences. Rules may vary by colony depending on the conservative or liberal leanings of the group. These rules may include no cars (although trucks are allowed because they assist in the work, not the pleasure of the colony), no radios, televisions, or magazines. "If we allowed the radio," said one minister, "our people would listen to the world and would soon be like it."[5]

The Hutterite baptism follows several years of training. Young people between the ages of twenty and thirty years old are baptized. At their baptism they accept the Apostles Creed as truth and promise ever to remain faithful to the colony.

The Dining Hall

The dining hall is one of the more important buildings in the colony since all meals are eaten as a group. On entering the building, one is greeted with the fine aroma of freshly baked bread. Women spend many hours preparing the meals in a large kitchen. The noon meal is the main meal of the day. Children between the ages of five and fifteen enter the dining hall first, ready for a break from their morning studies. They are ushered into their own separate dining room called the *Essenschuel* or "eating school" where they are served first. Here they are under the supervision of the *Schuellehrer* or "school teacher" and his wife. The adult dining hall is a large open room neatly set with long tables. Men sit on one side and women on the other. All meals begin and end in a German table prayer (or English if visitors are present) spoken by the pastor. First the women bring out the food to serve to the men. Then they return to the kitchen to get their plates filled. A typical noon dinner might consist of boiled chicken, French fries, soup, and a wide variety of home grown vegetables.

Hutterite Education

Hutterites believe that a good education is necessary to deal with the world around them. Although much learning takes place in the Hutterite homes, the colony does provide an organized system of education. Between the ages of two and a half and five, young Hutterite children receive a kindergarten education taught by the mothers of the colony. Here they enjoy singing, memory work, praying, and playtime. From age six to about fifteen, they attend a regular public school or the Hutterite taught school within the colony. Children are taught both German (*Hutterisch*) and English. Hutterite children are not educated to better themselves or to become successful in life. Rather they are taught how to become a useful part of their Bruderhof. Obedience is always stressed throughout their schooling. One Hutterite said, "After they learn obedience, they can be taught the faith".[6]

Today many Hutterite teachers receive a university education. In 1994 a new program for Hutterite teachers began at Brandon University in Manitoba, Canada. The Brandon University Hutterian Education Project was instituted to train Hutterites for classroom teaching. Those enrolled in the program attend university classes throughout the summer months and train in a classroom the remainder of the year.

Hutterite Farming and Commerce

Hutterite colonies usually farm huge tracts of land. Since the average Bruderhof has a population of 60 to 160 people, vast amounts of land are necessary to raise the produce needed to support them. It is not unusual to find a colony farming 10,000 acres or more. Livestock may include 100 cows, 1000 hogs, and 50,000 turkeys.[7] Their expertise at farming is well known and often envied by other area farmers and ranchers. Hutterites are not against the use of the latest in farming equipment. It is a common sight to see several huge prairie tractors parked side by side, along with combines and other major farm equipment, poised for work. Produce is used by the colony, shared with other colonies, or sold to the public. Monies received are kept in a common treasury and designated for daily expenses, building programs, or purchasing new farm land when the colony grows too large. At that point the colony is forced to divide and lots are cast to determine who will remain and who will leave for the new location.

Most colonies also conduct a second business in addition to farming. Furniture making, printing, book binding, or other professions bring additional revenue into the Bruderhof. Where there are many colonies in a settlement, each colony concentrates on a different vocation.

There is always a need for complete cooperation within the colony. Each man is trained in one area of colony work. Young men shadow their elders as they learn how to care for the pigs, finish cabinetry, or manage the farming. Occupations are assigned and there is no salary for any work done. Whatever someone needs is provided from the common treasury. Hutterites believe that surrendering one's life to Christ includes surrendering the human will plus all material goods. At baptism, the Hutterite takes a vow not to entertain any desire of owning property, for they believe that ownership is against the will of God. At most, families may receive a small token allowance of a few dollars for some necessities.

Hutterite Women

Colony women have a role subordinate to that of the men, although they are well cared for and respected by the men. The women are assigned to working groups which carry out particular chores. Their assignments may change periodically so that every woman shares in the daily routines of cooking, baking, laundry, canning, painting, cleaning, and teaching the little children. Sometimes the position of head cook, designated to oversee all the daily menus, is filled by an elected individual, and often the pastor's wife manages the sewing tasks of the colony. The woman's life is hard, but considered a joy since she is always surrounded by her colony sisters. Loneliness is seldom a problem in the commune because there is sufficient help for mothers to give birth, raise the children or travel to town.

Courtship and Marriage

One might think that young Hutterite men and women have few opportunities for courtship, but they claim that is not the case. Although years ago the mates were often chosen by the parents, today young Hutterites have ample opportunity to travel to neighboring colonies and meet other young Hutterites. Purity is stressed among the Hutterites and discipline for impure sexual relationships is severe. Many Hutterites practice an "open door" policy that says during courtship a couple will never be left alone behind closed doors. Courtship may be long or short, depending on their baptism. Most Hutterites are baptized in their early twenties, and marriage may not take place until both the young man and young woman are baptized.

Weddings are often held after a Sunday morning worship service. The young couple is asked to step forward and repeat a "yes" to the marriage promises. The day's dinner will likely include some celebration extras. Following the dinner meal there may be group singing, but by evening the celebrating gives way to the normal daily routine. Wine and beer may be served at some Hutterite weddings, a tradition dating back to the days when the Hutterites of Ukraine were allowed to produce their own wine. But excessive drinking is met with harsh punishment or even excommunication. The newlyweds live in the house of the groom's parents or are furnished with their own apartment.

The Hutterite Family

Hutterite family life is much different from that in western culture. In Hutterite practice, families are second to the importance of the Bruderhof. Although families each have a private residence, children and parents spend little time together during the day since dining and worship is always carried on in separation. There is great respect for the elderly. Children and grandparents spend quality time together since Hutterite men may retire from required labor at about age fifty, although they often work at less demanding jobs so they can continue to be contributing members of the colony.

The bond within a colony is very strong and few defect from it. Although times are changing and more young people are leaving the colonies, it is still estimated that fewer than 1% leave permanently. Because there are so few converts into the Hutterite religion, all Hutterites share about fifteen last names. Detailed records have been kept of each family line dating back to their days in Europe.

Sports and Leisure

Although the more conservative colonies may discourage or even prohibit any form of sports, many Hutterite colonies allow their young people to enjoy sports activities such as soccer, ice hockey, baseball, and volleyball. Young ladies enjoy rug making, flower arranging, and other crafts. Hutterites are also well known for their love of singing. Many colonies have excellent youth choirs who perform their four-part a cappella songs at nursing homes, hospitals and in other neighboring colonies. Selections include German songs as well as Gospel hymns. Some colonies have even marketed recordings by their youth choirs.

Hutterite Dress

As with all other areas of their lives, Hutterites follow a strict dress code in keeping with the colony Ordnung. Typically, men wear suspenders, black trousers, and plaid or plain buttoned shirts. Married men usually grow a beard.

Women wear their dresses below the knee. The younger girls usually wear brighter colored dresses than do the older women. Women always keep their heads covered with a dark scarf. Girls wear a *Mutze* or bonnet cap on their heads. Girls and women may not cut their hair and must put their hair up each day in the traditional Hutterite fashion of rolling the hair in front and coming together in a bun on the back.

Hutterites Today

Beside the Dariusleut, Lehrerleut, and divided Schmiedeleut, another group, the Arnoldleut, is also associated with the Hutterites. (This group is also known as The Bruderhof or The Society of Brethren. Today The Bruderhof sponsors a company known as Community Playthings that produces high-quality children's play equipment.) This group, originating in Germany in the 1930's, was led by Eberhard Arnold. Arnold began a commune that held beliefs similar to the Hutterian Brethren. Arnold lived with a Hutterite colony for a year and was ordained a Hutterian minister. In 1990 a major rift took place between the Hutterites and the Arnoldleut. The former accused the Arnoldleut of teaching millennialism, joining protest marches, taking a lawsuit to court, entertaining at a wedding with musical instruments, and baptizing by immersion. Because of these controversies, the Hutterites excommunicated the Arnoldleut and asked that they stop using the Hutterite name.[8] Today there are a few Arnoldleut churches still located in the state of New York.

Hutterites today are seeing the need for outreach programs. They now realize the importance of reaching out to surrounding communities and the world. Although they live in a closed society, they stress being good neighbors and showing care and concern for their local communities. Some Hutterite groups have begun mission work in Nigeria, Haiti, Japan, and Romania where they supervise orphanages and local building programs.

With over 400 years of hostility and hatred behind them, today's Hutterites enjoy a relatively peaceable existence in northern United States and Canada. Perhaps their temporal journey has ended.

1. William E. Estep, *The Anabaptist Story*, p. 103.
2. Cornelius J. Dyck, *An Introduction to Mennonite History*, p. 242.
3. http://mtprof.msun.edu/Spr1993.TBP.html
4. http://hutterites.org/organiz.htm.
5. John A. Hostetler, *Hutterite Life*, p. 21.
6. Ibid., p. 26.
7. Donald B. Kraybill, *Anabaptist World USA*, p. 95
8. http://www.perefound.org.html.1

CHAPTER 4
Menno Simons Takes Over

Not all Plain People we see along the back roads are Hutterites or Amish. There is a small group of Mennonites who also live in the style of the Plain People. Old Order Mennonites can be found on the back roads in the Midwest, in Pennsylvania and along the Atlantic coast. Although they represent only about 5% of the entire Mennonite population, the Old Order Mennonites sometimes receive the most attention because of their lifestyle.

The Mennonites are both the largest Anabaptist group and the most diverse. Mennonites cover the entire spectrum of Anabaptism, from the traditional Old Order groups (5%), to the moderate groups (25%), to the more liberal groups (70%). We can piece together more of our Anabaptist puzzle by taking a close look at the history behind the Mennonite Church.

Mayhem at Münster

It would be difficult to present Mennonite history without taking a long look at the city that stands at the beginning of the Mennonite timeline, although by no means as a positive role model. The following account is somewhat detailed, yet it does present an interesting moment in time for the Anabaptist movement. To witness the birth of the Mennonites we will travel north into the Netherlands, where a large number of people were converted to the Anabaptist faith.

Driving the Back Roads

The Netherlands suffered under the rule of the Spanish King, who also happened to be the Holy Roman Emperor. Floods, plague, desperate living conditions, and confusion over a number of Bible translations made these people prime mission targets. Melchior Hoffmann was one of the first to realize this, and during his career he sent missionaries there. A former furrier with no theological background, Hoffmann appointed himself to be leader and savior. He soon became an energetic evangelist and preacher. Hoffmann was an early follower of Martin Luther, but Luther himself said that Hoffmann should be silenced.[1] Hoffmann later sought friendship with Zwingli, who likewise rebuffed him. Hoffmann lived in Strassburg, France, where his egotistical ways led him down a dismal path of speculation and prophecy. Convinced that he held the true interpretation of the Bible, Hoffmann soon persuaded his followers that Strassburg was chosen by God as the New Jerusalem and that he was appointed by God to be the new Elijah, the forerunner of Christ's second coming. Even the date and time of Christ's return was predicted. In 1533 Hoffmann prophesied that he would be arrested, serve six months in prison, and return as the glorious new leader of the people. However it didn't take long for him to realize that his calculations missed the mark. As predicted, he was arrested, but weeks of imprisonment turned into months and the months turned into years. Melchior Hoffmann died in prison in 1543, ten years after his arrest. Today even the Anabaptists have little respect for the man they label as the "Anabaptist Enthusiast".[2]

But Hoffmann's legacy continued with the missionaries he sent to Holland. In 1533 Hoffmannite Jan Mathijs became a formidable preacher in Amsterdam. He sent out missionaries to convert those in the surrounding provinces. One such city was Münster in northern Germany. The 15,000 citizens were already in religious turmoil. Two years earlier a former priest, Bernard Rothmann, was converted by Luther's Reformation and immediately became a Lutheran pastor. Within a year, all the churches of Münster began to follow the new movement, with the exception of the Catholic cathedral. However, before long Rothmann began denying infant baptism which led to his dismissal. Soon Anabaptist-like beliefs were beginning to swirl through the streets of Münster. Yet Rothmann was just setting the stage for something the people of Münster would never forget. The Anabaptist invasion was about to begin!

When Jan Mathijs received word that Münster was vulnerable to the Anabaptist doctrine, he moved there to carry out Hoffmann's dreams. Mathijs first claimed that God had changed his mind and declared that the New Jerusalem was Münster instead of Strassburg, and that he was appointed by God to be the new Enoch. He also proclaimed that the people must prepare for Christ's second coming by destroying all wickedness within the city walls. "Rebaptize or leave" was the new message being preached by Mathijs and his followers.

As expected, the Catholic bishop could not tolerate this rebellion. For eighteen months he positioned his troops around the city walls and laid siege to it. Within the city, the people were rapidly turning to Anabaptism. Laborers, leaders, and even monks and nuns were being swept away by the excitement that was overtaking the city. To add to the fray, a twenty-five year old enthusiast and follower of Mathijs, Jan van Leiden arrived and began proclaiming himself as an appointed apostle of God. By February, 1534, the Anabaptists began to march through the city with armed soldiers. They seized a few town cannons and paraded through the streets singing, praying and shouting that the angels of heaven were about to descend on the town to deliver God's saints.

Rothmann issued a letter to the surrounding cities:
"God has made known to us that all should get ready to go to the new Jerusalem, the City of the Saints, because he is going to punish the world."[3]

Soon the city was filled with people of all sorts. Some filed through the streets shouting "Repent and be baptized! Slay the un-baptized heathen!" while others threw themselves on the ground stretching out their arms in the form of a cross, shouting out curses to all who did not follow their teaching.

Mathijs continued as leader, claiming that Münster was divined to be the city of saints that could withstand all the powers of the devil. When he appeared before the people, he carried two tablets of stone and claimed he received special direction from the Lord of Hosts. With the town completely under his control, Mathijs next declared a new election of the city council. With this election the once pacifist Anabaptists began wearing a new hat of political control and absolute rule by the sword.

On February 27, 1535, a decree was issued that all inhabitants must either be re-baptized or face being killed or driven out of the city. The Anabaptist contingent armed themselves with muskets and swords as they paraded through the streets searching out the "heathen". Those who agreed to be rebaptized were ushered into the town square where the new converts signed their names to a register and bowed their heads to be baptized.

New coins were minted and the entire population was required to wear special necklaces with tokens depicting Scripture passages. Dissent was handled severely. The story is told of one local smith named Ruscher who wrote that the leaders acted as if they were possessed by the devil. The following day he was ushered before the assembly where he was sentenced to death by Jan van Leyden and Jan Mathijs. Fear reigned within the city, while the siege outside the city walls was also finding some success. Soon the radical leaders collected all the money, silver and gold and placed it in a common treasury to be used as the leaders saw fit.

Jan Mahijs was the first to die. One day while attending a meeting, he threw up his hands, rose up and kissed each one present saying "God's peace be with you all." The following day he led a small band of soldiers outside the city intending to raid those laying siege to the town. In the skirmish that ensued Mathijs was killed. His head was removed and his body was cut into small pieces as the bishop's soldiers shouted that the Anabaptists could now come out beyond the city gates and receive their fallen leader.

The town was about to be thrown into even deeper turmoil as Jan van Leyden anointed himself King David, ruler over the New Israel and king over all the earth. Mathijs had been more extreme than Hoffmann, but van Leyden went even further. A new city constitution was drawn up that placed the town under the guidance of twelve elders, named after the twelve tribes of Israel. All life within the city walls of Münster was to be modeled after the Old Testament. This included the introduction of polygamy. Since many of the male citizens had left for fear of losing their lives, there was an overabundance of women and van Leyden made it compulsory for every woman to be married.

Van Leyden appeared before the people dressed in royal robes and a gold crown crafted especially for him. He wore gold chains and a sheathed sword decorated with the finest jewels. The widow of the late Jan Mathijs, now the wife of van Leyden, was crowned as queen. Wherever they went throughout the city, they were heralded with the blast of trumpets. His entourage included beautiful horses and two pages, one carrying a sword of justice and the other the books of the Old Testament.

By the end of 1534, the famine had become serious. Houses were searched for any food that might be concealed from the city fathers. Yet van Leyden was confident that God would rescue the town. The towers of St. Lamberti Church, the town's tallest cathedral, were used to keep twenty-four hour surveillance on the enemy camped outside the city walls. All other churches were renamed and all Catholic rites and observances were stripped from the town records.

By late spring 1535, as the Catholic bishop tightened the siege on the city, people began dying from lack of food. Horses were slaughtered and eaten and every available plot of ground was cultivated and planted. But it was too little too late. Finally van Leyden opened a four day window allowing anyone who wished to flee to safety to do so. Scores left, although many were met with instant death at the hands of the soldiers outside the city. Meanwhile food became even more scarce. In May, van Leyden issued a decree to evacuate the city of all women and children. This included van Leyden's fourteen wives, with only the queen staying behind.

The siege had been effective but was not able to end the occupation of Münster. Weapons were at a premium. Finally, in May, 1535, with the help of several neighboring provinces, the bishop was able to amass a fair size contingent of soldiers. On the 21st of May scaling ladders were placed against the walls, and before long the sleeping Anabaptists found themselves occupied by their enemy. The Anabaptists stood arm in arm in the town marketplace, just a block from the famed St. Lamberti Church. But by the middle of the next day the city was again under the control of the Catholic bishop.

A court was set up to try the defenders. All who remained true to the Anabaptist teaching were killed, including the queen of Jan van Leyden, who was beheaded in the town square. But a far worse sentence awaited the leaders of the revolt. Van Leyden and two of his closest advisers were captured, tortured, and put to death. The dream of a New Zion had come to a bloody end. The remains of the three Anabaptist radicals were put into iron cages and hung from the towers of St. Lamberti for all to see. Over the years, the towers have been replaced, however, even today three iron cages are still suspended from the steeple of St.

Lamberti church to remind the people of Münster of the Anabaptist takeover.

The days of the militant Anabaptists had come to a bloody end. It was a time of regret and distaste, a time when lust for power blinded a peaceful people to the point of murder and destruction.

Menno Simons Takes Control

While the Münster calamity was at center stage, a young Catholic priest named Menno Simons was beginning his break with the Catholic Church. In staunch disagreement with the real presence of the body and blood in the Lord's Supper, and seeing no scriptural basis for infant baptism, Menno declared himself separated from the Catholic Church. Upon hearing of the death of his brother Peter, who died furthering the cause of the Anabaptist revolution at Münster, Menno realized that the Anabaptists needed internal guidance. The Anabaptist cause was out of control under the leadership of a few uneducated zealots who had sadly led scores of people to their untimely deaths. The Dutch Anabaptists needed to find the right path, and Menno was not afraid to point out their errors and misgivings as he traveled from town to town. By 1536 Menno Simons had accumulated a large following of faithful Anabaptists. Soon the Dutch and north German Anabaptists who followed his leadership became known as Mennists or Mennonists–eventually settling on the term Mennonites. The Anabaptists of Switzerland, however, retained the name Swiss Brethren, although both factions were in agreement with the teachings and writings of Simons. Ironically, in later years the Dutch Anabaptists began to call themselves simply "Baptist-minded", while the Swiss Brethren proudly took upon themselves the name of Mennonites. Menno Simons was perhaps the most influential leader in the Anabaptist movement.

William Penn's "Holy Experiment"

As the history of the struggling Anabaptists continued, it came to an interesting intersection where church history and American history crossed paths. This began with a simple dream in the mind of a man revered in most American history books. The colony of New Amsterdam (New York) was visited by the Dutch Mennonites in 1644 for the purpose of commerce, but not to establish a new home. In 1663 however, forty-one Dutch Mennonites settled in Delaware, yet their settlement lasted only about a year, ending during the Anglo-Dutch War.

The first permanent settlement took place in 1683 when a group of Mennonites from northern Germany found their way to Germantown, Pennsylvania. This area would eventually become the most popular area for Anabaptist settlements.

This came about because of an adventursome young Quaker named William Penn. Penn was schooled at the prestigious Oxford University. In 1665 Penn's father took him to Ireland to avoid the plague. There he met Thomas Loe, a Quaker (Society of Friends) preacher. Penn was impressed with Loe's teaching, and in a few years Penn himself became a prominent Quaker preacher. He was influential in the Quaker movement and has several theological works to his credit. Since the Quakers refused to become subject to the Church of England they were persecuted. Like the Anabaptists, the Quakers also refused military service and dressed in plain clothing. Penn himself was imprisoned for several months for his Quaker beliefs.

But it was not this William Penn who was ultimately responsible for the creation of Pennsylvania. Rather, it was his father, Admiral Sir William Penn, who is really to be credited with the land purchase. When Admiral Penn died, King Charles II still owed him a sizable amount of back pay. On hearing about the debt, young William suggested that in place of the money, the King would grant him a plot of land west of the

Delaware River in the New World. In 1681 his wish was granted, and "Penn's Woods" or Pennsylvania became a reality.

William Penn wanted a place where many religions would exist side by side in tolerance of one another. Love would be the guiding force in their government. He called his plan the "Holy Experiment."

Penn spent considerable time traveling throughout Europe advertising his new colony. There are records of at least three instances in the late 1600's when Penn traveled throughout northern Germany boasting about the new land across the sea that offered peace for persecuted people like the Anabaptists. A few Mennonites in search of religious freedom settled near Philadelphia in 1683. Soon more Mennonites settled in the Lancaster County area. There were four major migrations among the Anabaptists. The first and largest migration of between 3000 to 5000 Mennonites and Amish settled there in the early to mid 1700's. Most settlers preferred the rich soil of Lancaster County. Many of these Mennonites were of the Old Order group.

> **WILLIAM PENN'S CONSTITUTION OF GOVERNMENT**
>
> "...that all persons living in the province who confess and acknowledge the Almighty and Eternal God to be Creator, Upholder and Ruler of the world–subject to the general rules of piety, all are welcome. Only those who denied the existence of God should be excluded."[5]

A second wave of about 3000 Amish began after the Revolutionary War in the early 1800's. These settled mostly in Indiana, Ohio, and Illinois and many have since joined the Mennonites.

A third group of several hundred Mennonites arrived in the New World in the mid 1800's. Many of these moved directly to Indiana, and today are part of the Mennonite Conference and Old Order Mennonites.

The fourth migration took place shortly after the Civil War, settling in Ohio, Indiana, North Dakota, and Canada. Many of these were Hutterites who had lived in Russia. By 1900 there were no Hutterites or Amish living in Europe. The land that held the graves of their ancestors was completely forsaken in their seemingly endless search for a peaceful home. Estimates claim a total of about 8000 Anabaptists sailed the Atlantic Ocean to begin a new home for their church families.

A Dangerous Journey

For this group of persecuted believers from Europe, the dangers and hardships of their move to America are almost beyond imagination. To begin, money was scarce, and many of the fares were paid by church members who remained in Europe. Many weeks were spent simply trying to reach the port of departure in Rotterdam. For travelers from southern Germany, such a trip could take a month and a half, being stopped repeatedly at the dozens of check points and customs stations along the way, many of which charged exorbitant rates for passage. They would set sail at Rotterdam for a three month journey to Philadelphia. It's difficult to imagine the "stench, fumes, horror, vomiting, and many kinds of sickness" these people had to bear. Lice were so plentiful; they could be scraped from their bodies. Many claimed they were packed "like herring" on these ill-fated voyages. Estimates claim as many as one-half of the travelers met their death at sea.[6]

The following is an excerpt from S. Duane Kaufman's *"Miscellaneous Documents"* from the *Pennsylvania Mennonite Heritage 2,* July, 1979. This record was likely written in 1737 aboard the *Charming Nancy*, a ship carrying Amish passengers:

"The 28th of June while in Rotterdam getting ready to start my Zernbli died and was buried in Rotterdam. The 29th we got under sail and enjoyed one and a half days of favorable wind. The 7th of July, early in the morning, Hans Zimmerman's son-in-law died.

"We landed in England the 8th of July, remaining nine days in port during which five children died. Went under sail the 17th of July. The 21st of July my own Lisbetli died. Several days before Michael Georgli had died.

"On the 29th of July three children died. On the first of August my Hansli died and the Tuesday previous five children died. On the 3rd of August contrary winds beset the vessel and from the 1st to the 7th of the month three more children died. On the 8th of August, Shamblien's Lizzie died and on the 9th Burgli's child died. Passed a ship on the 21st. A favorable wind sprang up. On the 28th Hans Gasli's wife died. Passed a ship the 13th of September.

"Landed in Philadelphia on the 18th and my wife and I left the ship on the 19th. A child was born to us on the 20th–died–wife recovered. A voyage of eighty-three days."[7]

The Mennonites Today

The Mennonites today are an extremely diversified church. Because of the wide range of Mennonites, from conservative to liberal, it is difficult to focus on one specific group. It is estimated that worldwide there are more than one million Mennonites. In North America alone there are about forty different Mennonite denominations, the largest being the Mennonite Church USA, with over 150,000 baptized members. One of the reasons for the large number of denominations stems from their history.

Most Mennonites trace their heritage to one of two groups: the Swiss-German Mennonites and the Dutch-Russian Mennonites. In the early years, persecuted Mennonites sought refuge in the Netherlands. However, some groups migrated to Russia at the invitation of Catherine the Great.

The Dutch Mennonites were eventually asked to join William Penn in his "Holy Experiment" in Pennsylvania in the late 1600's. This was the first group to cross the sea for a new beginning. In the early 1900's, when Russia placed heavy restrictions on the Mennonites living there, the Russian Mennonites also moved to America. However, instead of settling in Pennsylvania, most of the Russian Mennonites moved to north central United States and Canada.

The Mennonites today vary widely in their teaching and lifestyles. On the conservative end are the Old Order Mennonites who live similar to the Amish. These represent about 5% of the total Mennonites in North America. The middle group is comprised of the moderate Mennonites. These live modern lives, but still retain many of the old traditions and dress. About 25% of the Mennonite world is moderate. The remaining 70% live in the modern world and are considered the most liberal of the Anabaptist churches.

Old Order Mennonites

Unlike their Amish cousins, the Old Order Mennonites can only trace their history back to the days of the Civil War. In 1872 a large group of Mennonites in northern Indiana and Ohio protested the many new innovations that were finding their way into the church. Practices like Sunday school, evening worship, foreign missions, and the use of English were all beginning to infiltrate their churches. One group of Mennonites refused to change. They wished to reclaim what they felt was the true essence of the Mennonite church. They believed that the church should return to its old culture and old Ordnungs. Eventually they broke apart from the more liberal Mennonites and took on the name of Old Order Mennonites. Since then, the Old Order has again divided into several conferences. The larger Groffdale Conference (also called Wenger Mennonites or Team Mennonites–as in a "team of horses") live mostly in the Lancaster, Pennsylvania, area although Ohio and Wisconsin also claim some Groffdale Conference Mennonites. They are especially known for their continued use of the horse and buggy.

> **THE MENNONITE CHURCH**
> (Largest bodies)
>
> **CONSERVATIVE (5%)**
> Old Order Mennonites 13,000 people
> Weaverland Conference
> (1893 Pennsylvania)
>
> Groffdale Conference 16,000 people
> (1893 Lancaster, Pennsylvania)
>
> Old Colony Mennonites 1000 people
> (1977 Canada & Mexico)
>
> **MODERATES (25%)**
> Church of God in Christ Mennonites
> (1859) 12,000 people
> Conservative Mennonite Conference
> (1910 Pigeon, Michigan) 19,000 people
>
> **LIBERALS (70%)**
> Mennonite Church USA
> (2002) 160,000 people
> Mennonite Brethren Church
> (1860 Russia) 30,000 people[8]

Their buggies take on an interesting array of styles and designs, from the open-topped buggies that the young people decorate with elaborate pin striping, decals and reflectors, to the very conservative black covered buggies that have no side or back windows.[9] These conservative Mennonites live much like their Amish relatives, with only slight differences in clothing, church structure and some Ordnung rules that are enforced by the chosen leaders.

One Old Order member explained that there are five levels of moral conduct: Level one consists of the behaviors that are acceptable such as eating an ice cream cone, kissing one's spouse, wearing shoes or playing softball. The second step is made up of mild taboos that they just will not partake in such as riding in a hot air balloon, wearing a wristwatch, or using cosmetics. The third level is those things which are "testified against" by the church but are not a test of membership. These might include owning stylish furniture, going on a pleasure trip, or receiving Social Security. As one bishop put it, "good members just don't do these things". The next step includes forbidden behaviors such as joining the military or owning a television. These are punishable by excommunication from the church. The fifth and final level speaks to those things forbidden by the Bible such as drunkenness, divorce, swearing oaths, or fornication. Because these are forbidden in the Bible, they are not named in their church Ordnung. Usually the Ordnung addresses those morals required in level three and four.[10]

Like the Amish, the Groffdale Mennonites have large families with between eight and twelve children. Their retention rate is 80% and may be as high as 95% in some church districts.

The smaller Weaverland Conference allows the use of cars. For many years they were known as the Black Bumper Mennonites because they repainted their chrome bumpers black. Today only the pastors drive black-bumpered automobiles, while the other church members drive dark colored cars and vans. This conference also conducts English worship services although having a Sunday school is still in question.[11]

Moderate Mennonites

Twenty or so groups comprise the moderate arm of the Mennonites. This group is made up of rural members who, for whatever reason wished to modernize, and from those who felt that the main body of the Mennonite church has drifted into the liberal arena. These people still dress plain, and elect lay ministers as do the Amish and Hutterites, yet they are not against using electricity or having telephones in their homes. However, they do not allow televisions, radios, and computers. They are very strict in their view of excommunication and in their opposition to divorce and ordination of women.

The Main Body of the Mennonite Church

The largest part of the Mennonite church was previously called the Old Mennonite Church (not to be confused with the Old Order Mennonites). This group traces its history back to the Swiss-German immigrants who settled in Pennsylvania. Today this

> **TEN THOUSAND VILLAGES**
>
> The Mennonites today operate stores called Ten Thousand Villages that sell handcrafted items made by people in their mission villages around the world.

church is spread throughout the world and claims members who are Latinos, African-Americans, and Asians of Hmong, Laotian, and Vietnamese descent. Many Mennonites serve as missionaries around the world.

After twenty years of planning and meeting, in February, 2002, the two largest Mennonite denominations, The Mennonite Church and the General Conference Mennonite Church, joined to form the Mennonite Church USA. Today that church claims more than half of the Mennonites in the world.

The German Baptist Brethren

Although not part of the Mennonite church, there is one other group that deserves attention, the German Baptist Brethren who began in the early 1700's. This group was not directly descended from the original Swiss Anabaptists, but they sympathized with Anabaptist teachings. The German Baptist Brethren began in 1708, and was made up of German Lutheran and Reformed believers who became disenchanted with what they perceived as a lack of spirituality in their churches. These so-called "Radical Pietists" or "Separatists" called for complete separation from the official churches. They emphasized the importance of the Love Feast and adult baptism. The Love Feast sometimes lasted for two days and included foot washing, extensive hymn singing, communion, multiple sermons and the "holy kiss of charity" on the cheek. Because they believed in triple immersion, they became known as the Dunkards, Tunkards, or simply Dunkers. Today the Brethren churches have a total population of about 300,000.[12]

BRETHREN CHURCHES
(Largest Brethren groups)

Old German Baptist Brethren (1881)
The Brethren Church (1883)
Church of the Brethren (1908)
Dunkard Brethren (1926)
Grace Brethren (1939)
(Not all churches who call themselves Brethren are connected with this group.)

Driving the Back Roads

1. Donald B. Kraybill, *On the Backroad to Heaven*, p. 152.
2. Publication Board of the Eastern Pennsylvania Mennonite Church, *The Swiss Anabaptists*, p. 71.
3. Anthony Arthur, *The Taylor King*, p. 61.
4. Ibid, p. 187
5. http://www.libertyhaven.com.
6. Publication Board of Eastern Pennsylvania Mennonite Church, *The Swiss Anabaptists*, p. 93.
7. Steven M. Nolt, *A History of the Anabaptists*, p. 47.
8. Donald B. Kraybill, *Anabaptist World USA*, p. 158 ff.
9. Stephen Scott, *Plain Buggies*, p. 81.
10. Donald B. Kraybill, *On the Backroad to Heaven*, p. 74, 75.
11. Ibid, p. 65.
12. Donald B. Kraybill, *Anabaptist World USA*, p. 79.

CHAPTER 5
Amish Riddles

As we travel the back roads of Amish country, we discover a culture that seems to make little sense. Everyone who passes a horse and buggy, catches a glimpse of blue trousers lined up on the clothesline, or sees a team of work horses straining with a plow, no doubt has asked the same question: why? The riddle of the Amish is difficult to understand because society has trained us to think differently than they do. To understand the Amish way of life means we must first begin to view ourselves from a completely different vantage point because it is the Amish way of thinking that lies at the root of the Amish way of living. We will now add three more pieces into our puzzle labeled "Jacob Ammann", "Gelassenheit", and "Ordnung", all necessary to help us complete the Anabaptist puzzle.

Jacob Ammann Disagrees

The Amish were the last of the three main Anabaptist groups to form. The first rebaptism by Manz, Blaurock, and Grebel took place in 1525, the Hutterites were born in 1527, and Menno Simons began the formal Mennonite movement in 1536. It took another 157 years for the Amish to become a major player in the Anabaptist church.

Unlike the other Anabaptist branches that grew out of the Reformation era, the Amish arose from problems within the Anabaptist movement. In the summer of 1693, a young, zealous,

Swiss Anabaptist elder named Jacob Ammann began visiting neighboring congregations in the Alsace region. There were several problems that he felt needed to be addressed. The first was the frequency of celebrating Holy Communion. The Anabaptists observed Holy Communion once every year. They claimed that since Jesus celebrated the Feast of the Passover (where he instituted Holy Communion) once every year, so once a year should be sufficient for them. Ammann proposed twice each year. His reason was that believers would have to carefully examine themselves on two occasions, and that would serve to strengthen their faith.

Second, Ammann questioned the current practice of excommunication. Whereas the Swiss Anabaptists believed in excommunication or the ban as defined by the Schleitheim Articles, Ammann wanted to follow more closely the teachings of the Dordrecht Confession which taught that the impenitent would not only be excommunicated, but would also face shunning, or *Meidung*. A person who was shunned would be forbidden from public worship, and he or she would be considered an outcast and would be banned from all social dealings. This ban included family get-togethers, and contact for business purposes. Ammann insisted that shunning must be followed to uphold the integrity of the church. Shunning would be carried out for any family member, be it son or daughter, husband or wife. (Amish are taught to report one another if they step outside the rules of the church in general, or if they transgress the rules of the Ordnung.) After a person has been found guilty, or has left the church, plans for the excommunication and shunning begin. Once these are in place, a person may return to the colony, but will usually be met with a chorus of discipline. In her book, *Crossing Over,* Ruth Irene Garrett, an Amish woman who ran away to marry an "English" man and is now a member of a Lutheran Church in Bowling

Green, Kentucky, wrote the following about her return to see her parents:

> "My biggest concern was that people would discover I was in town before I got a chance to see my family. That would have been disastrous. My father would have summoned a gaggle of ministers, and they would have confronted me, surrounded me with feelings of guilt, and hounded me into submission. Because that's what they do to fallen members of their flock. They badger them. Intimidate them. Shame them. And demand obedience. I would have been mortified."[1]

Third, Ammann felt that the practice of foot washing prior to the communion services must again be practiced. He claimed that just as Jesus washed the feet of the disciples prior to eating the Lord's Supper, so they must do the same today. In essence Ammann was attempting to bring the Mennonite church back to its conservative roots.

A fourth point of contention surfaced as discussions were being held. Jacob Ammann (himself a tailor by occupation), preached the importance of wearing traditional, plain clothing. This meant an end to following the grooming and clothing styles of the world. There was to be no more trimming of the beard or dressing in fashionable clothing. Because the Amish felt that buttons were too showy, they became known as the "hook and eyers", or *Haftler,* as opposed to the Mennonite "button people" or *Knopflers.*

The first several preachers that Ammann approached were at best lukewarm to his proposals, so Ammann immediately declared them excommunicated. Ammann was indeed serious about his quest, and he would stop at nothing to achieve the results he wanted. Soon this letter by Jacob Ammann made its way to the other Swiss Mennonite churches:

"Together with the other ministers and bishops, I, Jacob Ammann, am sending this writing to everyone who is not already expelled by judgment and resolution, both men and women, ministers and lay people, to inform you that you shall appear before us on or before February 20th to answer whether you can confess these controversial articles with us, namely: to avoid those who are expelled, and that no one shall be saved apart from the Word of God. If you can instruct us of a better way, from the Word of God, we shall lend you an ear....We shall appoint another date, namely March 7th, on which you may present your answer. But if you fail to appear, and answer at this appointed time, then you shall according to my teaching and creed, be expelled by us ministers and elders, especially by me, Jacob Ammann, as sectarians, and shall be shunned and avoided until the time of your repentance according to the Word of God. This paper shall be sent from one person to another to make it known to all. A.D. 1693."[2]

The result was a mass excommunication of both ministers and lay people in the Alsace region. Ammann retained about half the ministers as his supporters. Three years later, the Ammann or Amish group as it was now known, rescinded the excommunication and apologized for the hasty decision. In an attempt to reconcile their position, the Amish instead excommunicated themselves. By offering an olive branch, the two parties were able to finally meet, but with little success. The damage was done, and the rift would never be healed.

Today most Amish know very little about Jacob Ammann, perhaps because very few of his writings have been found. Preferring to regard themselves as Anabaptists, some Amish recognize Ammann as an embarrassment while others feel his work was necessary to right the wrongs that were beginning to infiltrate the Anabaptist church.

Gelassenheit

To begin understanding the Old Order churches it is first necessary to look at the philosophy and foundation that lies beneath this religion. This step can be difficult for anyone who is steeped in today's culture. Most Americans are taught to satisfy their own desires and ambitions. Students go on to higher education to get a good job and begin climbing the success ladder. Parents are taught to glorify their children for getting good grades, and achieving success in the arts or athletics. Schools distribute awards, medals, scholarships, ribbons, and certificates, all to glorify the student. The media is filled with a wide range of elixirs to help make us more attractive, from weight loss pills, to makeup, from muscle-building machines to new ways to grow hair. We are well-trained to become completely wrapped up in ourselves. Personal achievement has for many become the god.

This worldly approach is the complete opposite of how the Amish view their place on earth. Seldom discussed verbally, their philosophy of life is centered on the practice of Gelassenheit or yielding to a higher authority. This philosophy permeates their every thought and action. It involves the practice of *Demut* (humility) instead of *Hochmut* (pride). Although the German term Gelassenheit may be somewhat difficult to define precisely, one can get the gist of it by considering the synonyms: self-surrender, resignation to God's will, yielding to others, gentleness, a calm spirit, contentment, quiet acceptance of whatever comes, giving up one's will, calmness of mind, composure, conquest of selfishness, longsuffering, inner surrender, self-denial, submission.

Gelassenheit can be seen in the actions of Amish children as well as adults. The child learns that his toys are not his own, but belong to everyone in the family. Likewise the farmer must submit to every rule laid down by the church district. One Amish member put it this way, "The yielding and submitting is the core of our faith and relationship with God." This is demonstrated when young Amish men and women await their baptism. They sit in the front of the congregation with heads bowed and covered with their hands, demonstrating their willingness to submit their will to the greater good of the church district.

Author Donald Kraybill in his book *The Riddle of Amish Culture* describes how Gelassenheit rules every dimension of Amish character. He writes that the Amish personality is: reserved, modest, calm, quiet. The Amish values are: submission, obedience, humility, simplicity. Amish rituals include: kneeling, foot-washing, confession, shunning, and this can be seen in their symbolism: clothing, use of horses, buggies and German dialect. This philosophy can then be seen in their pacifist views, their refusal to take anyone to court, and their nonresistance to violence. One can sense it in the homes where there are no mirrors and where children are taught to keep their heads lowered when speaking with a stranger.[3]

The history of Gelassenheit dates back to the beginning of Anabaptist persecution. Instead of resisting and taking up arms against their captors, they willingly went to their deaths, which is the final expression of Gelassenheit. This showed their ultimate submission to God. (This is why the events at Münster were so atypical of the Anabaptists.)

> This is a favorite verse learned by Amish children that expresses Gelassenheit:
>
> I must be a Christian child,
>   Gentle, patient, meek, and mild;
> Must be honest, simple, true
>   In my words and actions too.
> I must cheerfully obey,
>   Giving up my will and way.
>
> Must remember, God can view
>   All I think, and all I do.
> Glad that I can know and try,
>   Glad that children such as I,
> In our feeble ways and small,
>   Can serve Him who loves us all.[4]

At an early age, Amish children are taught if they are to become children of God they must "give up" their will and obey.

Amish parents believe that the surest way to spoil children is to let them have their own way. They contend this encourages selfishness, disrespect, and covetousness. They maintain that unlike "modern" children who become spoiled by being ushered from event to event to help them discover their true selves, Amish children are busy washing dishes, feeding cows, pulling weeds, and mowing lawns–all for family and community. Children are taught the acronym J.O.Y.–Jesus first, You last, and Others in between.[5]

The Ordnung

Gelassenheit is not the only foundation for the Amish way of life. It would be useless if not consistent with the rules that follow the character established by Gelassenheit–the Ordnung, or "rules of discipline", that each church district establishes for itself and that governs the life of that church district. (A church district is a single congregation of members.)

The Ordnung originated with the Anabaptists in the 1700's as an outline of their faith. Since then it has become more a list of rules for the church members to follow. An Ordnung is not considered the law of God, but rather a list of rules or guidelines for daily living. These are the rules that give each church its distinctive character. The Ordnung is the backbone that supports the entire body of the Amish culture. They feel it reflects God's orderliness as opposed to the disorderliness of the world. Although unwritten, these rules are taught to Amish children from small on.

The purpose of the Ordnung is simple. The Amish believe that without a detailed set of rules the churches will lose their identity over time, and become inneffective. The Ordnung governs everything that would threaten their existence such as style of clothing, family life, worship, and education. When young Amish men or women get baptized, they promise never to forsake the Ordnung. If they do, they will be excommunicated and shunned. One Amish individual made the comment that baptism and shunning serve as the front and back door of Amish communities.

> "One is either in the church or on the outside. There is no happy medium. In spite of the outsider's view that the Ordnung is a law, a bondage of suppression, the person who has learned to live within a respectful church Ordnung appreciates its value. It gives freedom of heart, peace of mind, and a clear conscience. Such a person has actually more freedom, more liberty, and more privilege than those who would be bound to the outside."[6]

Ordnung rules established by each church vary from state to state or even district to district. Basically there are two types of regulations, those that were written years ago in the Dordrecht Confession of Faith and the Schleitheim Articles, and regulations for life established by each church. The confessional rules have been published for all to read and learn, but the individual church district regulations are passed down orally.

The church Ordnung guides the members in every area of Amish life and is designed to bring about a feeling of oneness. As the Amish follow each rule of dress, recreation, transportation, communication, farming, and home life, they establish a common pattern of life. One Amish woman said, "They [the Ordnung] are not meant to tell us what we are to do, just what we are *not* to do." Amish wish to be separate from the world. They prefer to be different. And in that difference they will all appear the same.

Several of the Ordnung rules are universal throughout the Old Order Amish church. These include no public electricity, no telephones, no central heating, no automobiles or tractors with air in the tires, no scissor or razor to touch a woman's body, beards for married men (but no mustaches), the use of horses for farming, and no education beyond eighth grade.

To these rules, a typical Ordnung may add the following:
Color and style of clothing

No bright, showy, form-fitting clothing. Colors such as red or orange are not permitted. Dresses are to be no shorter than midway between the floor and the knee. Outside pockets are allowed only on work pants and coats. Shoes are to be black and plain. Men must wear suspenders but without showy buckles. Women's heads must be covered at all times. Never any jewelry.

Hat styles for men

Hats are to be black with a specific size brim. Straw hats may be allowed in warmer months.

Hair style

Married men must grow a beard. Mustaches are not allowed because they resemble the facial hair worn by the soldiers at the time of the persecution. Men's and boys' hair is to be cut at mid-length of the ear. There is to be no part in the hair. Women may not cut their hair and must wear it up. Women may not shave their arms or legs.

Homes

No decorations inside or outside their buildings. No carpeting allowed inside the house–only linoleum or wood flooring is acceptable. No large mirrors, computers, radios, or televisions allowed. Curtains must be plain, never fancy. Embroidery is not allowed in the Amish home.

Education

No education beyond the eighth grade. Children are to be taught both German (incorrectly called Pennsylvania Dutch–it should be Pennsylvania Deutsch or German) and English.

Work
: Only horses are allowed for field work. Tractors may be used for the power drive to help with chores but not in the fields. No air-filled rubber tires.

Miscellaneous
: No musical instruments. No voting, running for office, or filing of lawsuits. No service in the military. Absolutely no divorce. No buying or selling on Sunday. No marriage until both individuals have been first baptized. Some Ordnung even include a ban on missionary work or any evangelism. The fear is that by meeting with the worldly in spiritual matters the Amish are putting their own souls in spiritual jeopardy.

Enterprising Amish have found ways to circumvent some of the Ordnung rules. For instance, although they cannot own an electric freezer, they can have "English" neighbors store Amish food in their freezers. Or although they cannot have a telephone inside their homes, they may have one in a booth at the end of the driveway.

The Ordnung is discussed prior to each communion service, at which time any new items may be added. One dissenter will not stop the rule from being instituted, but two nay votes will nullify any new ruling. Every member in the Amish community must express his or her complete agreement before the communion service will begin. After the rules are discussed, a woman walks through the group and asks each woman if she agrees while a male member does the same with the men. Everyone must answer that they agree to the rules.

To the outsider, the Ordnung may seem like merely a long list of rules and regulations, but for the Amish it is an important tool that unites the community and family members. One Amish minister put it this way, "The Ordnung generates peace, love, commitment, equality and unity...It creates a desire for togetherness and fellowship. It binds marriages, it strengthens family ties, to live together, to work together, to worship together, and to commune secluded from the world.[7]

But why? Why is a phone at the end of a driveway all right, but not inside the house? Why can the Amish run their machinery with a generator but not from the public electric power lines? Why is it acceptable for the Amish to ride in someone else's car, but not to own cars of their own? If we take a close look at these three areas of Amish life, we can begin to understand the purpose behind the Ordnung.

No Telephone

How could anyone possibly live without a telephone! Society has evolved from sharing a party line to the handy rotary dial desk phone, princess phone, pushbutton wall phone, wireless phone, to the ever present cell phone. What was once found only on the kitchen wall is now seemingly glued into the palms of adults, teens and even younger children. How is it possible that the Amish can avoid this "necessity"?

The use of the telephone has been on the front burner of Amish Ordnungs since the early 19th century and it is still forbidden by the conservative Old Order Amish. The telephone first appeared in Pennsylvania in the 1890's. The first reaction of the Amish Church was not to reject the new invention prompting many Amish families to have it installed in their homes. However by 1910 some problems became evident resulting in a quick ban on this new convenience. The reasons given were extensive: It was not a necessity, it contributed to pride and individualism, it came from the outside world, it was a detriment to face-to-face conversation, and it encouraged unmonitored private conversations and idle gossip. However the

Amish stopped short of banning total use of telephones–only those within the home.

Since the ban, the need for using the telephone has led to some very creative changes. Today's Amish homes may well have a phone in the workshop, or in a "telephone shanty" at the end of the driveway. With more and more Amish leaving farming and turning to home businesses, there is a greater need to have a telephone available. Local newspaper ads show listing after listing of Amish businesses giving a phone number beginning with "VM", meaning "voice mail". Whenever one calls these businesses, they will be greeted with a voice mail message stating their call will be returned at a later time. Sometimes the telephone shanty serves several families. There one might find a writing tablet where each user records his or her calls to help sort out the phone bills.

Today cell phones have only added to this confusion, as many Amish homes struggle with teenagers making private phone calls. Yet the Amish still try to remain true to their Ordnungs. "If we give in to the phone, what will be next?" one Amish adult wondered. The Amish are concerned that the telephone will only pull families apart, disunite the church, and cause general disintegration of their close-knit society. Up to now the phone agreement of telephone access but not in the homes still seems the best decision. How long it will last is yet to be seen.

No Cars

Anyone who has seen an Amish person step out of a car has wondered why the Amish can ride in cars but not drive or own one of their own? This riddle has followed the Amish for decades.

The Amish are not against using automobiles, trains and buses for transportation. (Airplane travel is not allowed.) Since the 1800's the Amish have agreed to ride in automobiles. They do, however, label the car a worldly luxury, and worldly things are not Amish things. One Amish remarked, "Anybody who gets a car just isn't Amish!" When the auto industry was in its very early years, the Amish had no opinion one way or the other about using cars. But before long the fledgling auto was regarded as the "king of sports and the queen of amusements".[8] That was not exactly what a people who disdained both sport and amusement wanted to hear. Soon the auto was seen only as a worldly toy for the wealthy.

By 1915 church districts began to vary in their views. Some allowed travel with neighbors, while others drew a line between business and pleasure. As more Amish searched for work outside of the farm, the need for transportation beyond the horse and carriage became a very real problem. Yet one reality still stood out above the rest, the automobile represented a means by which one could easily leave the confines of the Church district. This was not good, for it was through the closeness of the Amish community that they could continue their practice of separating themselves from the world. Once a community began to expand into the world, their very existence was at risk. Consequently Old Order districts drew a simple line. One would be allowed to ride in cars, but ownership was forbidden. To the Amish this was the practical answer to their problem.

No Electricity

Often the Amish became resourceful in their use of technology just to avoid breaking the rules of the Ordnung. Such was the case of using electricity. That the Amish reject any use of this public utility is no secret. They claim that increased use of televisions, radios, computers, and other connections with the outside world is a detriment to their society. Consequently, all Old Order Amish homes have ceiling hooks to hang their lanterns after the sun goes down. Homes are also free of the television chatter and loud radio or CD music that invades the peacefulness of many worldly homes. Yet what about other items that require electricity, such as electric fences, milk coolers, flashing carriage directional signals, and reading lights for the elderly? In each instance compromises consistent with the intent of Ordnung rules were worked out. While driving the back roads of Lancaster County, Pennsylvania, it was pointed out that one Amish family had public electricity lines entering a second floor room. This was allowed by the district because here lived a young Amish man on a respirator. Thus electricity was permitted, but only in that single room.

In the 1960's Amish farmers were pressed into storing their milk in coolers at the risk of losing their customers. The Hershey Company of Hershey, Pennsylvania, needed thousands of pounds of milk every day to produce their chocolate bars, and the Amish responded. As a result, today all Amish farms run generators to keep their milk cooler motors running. Likewise, it is not unusual to find propane-powered refrigerators in the Amish homes or generator driven tools in their workshops. Many Amish buggies have small 12 volt batteries installed in the undercarriage to provide enough power for the directional signals and the windshield wipers.

The Amish are careful to adjust to the times while not losing sight of the reason for their existence. Always willing to compromise yet never willing to give in, the Amish continue to walk a tightrope in a world of increased technology. One Amish person said, "Electric would lead to worldliness. What would come along with electric? All the things we don't need. With our diesel engines today we have more control of things. If you have an electric line coming in, then you'd want a full line of appliances on it. The Amish are human too, you know. It's not so much the electric that we're against, it's all the things that come with it–all the modern conveniences, television, computers. If we get electric lights, then where will we stop? The wheel [of change] would really start spinning then."[9]

1. Ruth Irene Garrett, *Crossing Over*, p. 3.
2. John A. Hotstetler, *Amish Society*, p. 37.
3. Donald B. Kraybill, *The Riddle of Amish Culture*, p. 31.
4. Donald B. Kraybill, *The Riddle of Amish Culture*, p. 30.
5. Poem provided by James E. Eshelman, Mount Joy, PA.
6. Donald B. Kraybill, *The Riddle of Amish Culture*, p. 34.
7. John A. Hostetler, *Amish Society*, p. 84.
8. Donald B. Kraybill, *The Riddle of Amish Culture*, p. 115.
9. Ibid, p. 201.

CHAPTER 6
The Amish at Worship

If you ever travel Amish back roads on a Sunday morning, it is possible you will see a bustle of activity as Amish buggies scurry into the driveway of one chosen farm. If you wait a few moments and strain your ears a bit, you may hear a strange chant begin as the congregation joins in a long, slow, unaccompanied German hymn. You are witnessing an Amish worship service– the same service you would have seen two hundred years ago. To better understand the puzzle of the Amish, we cannot overlook the importance of their worship life because it reflects the nature and character of the Amish people.

The Church District

It is important to understand that being Amish shows itself in everything they do. It is a way of life that sets them apart from everyone else. In a line up of a Catholic, a Methodist, a Baptist, a Lutheran and an Amish, there is little doubt who is the Amish. Why? Because the Amish are different. Their religion dictates their every move, and the foundation behind that move is found in their worship.

The Amish have no central church headquarters. Unlike most other Christian churches, the Amish do not have a synod office or central agency that operates programs for the church at large and keeps individual congregations informed. It is remarkable that a church body of nearly 200,000 members has maintained such a tight knit organization without any church bureaucracy. The basic Amish church structure is very simple. An individual Amish congregation is called a district or *Gemeinde*. A group of districts that are in fellowship with one another make up an affiliation.[1] Once a district grows to 200-250 members (20-40 families), a split takes place and a new district is formed. The district boundaries are determined by the church leaders and church members. Amish families must belong to the district within whose boundaries they reside. A large number of districts in a particular geographic area such as Lancaster County, Pennsylvania, or Holmes County, Ohio, comprise a settlement. Church districts within a settlement are often named by their location within the settlement, such as the North Church, or the Southeast Church.[2]

The Amish hold public worship once every two weeks. On off weeks the families either visit other church districts, or spend some time with relatives and friends. The Old Order Amish have no church buildings. They believe that the people are the church, not the building. Every able family in the district sponsors a Sunday church service sometime during the year. Many Amish design their homes with removable walls or extra large doorways to accommodate the worship services. If the house is too small, a cleaned shop or barn may also be used.

The host family must do a considerable amount of preparation. Not only must they provide a place for worship, they will also prepare a light meal for the 250 or so worshipers. Much of the burden is on the lady of the house, who along with the help of neighbors or relatives, must bake pies and prepare food for the Sunday afternoon luncheon. The meals are almost always the same; coffee, homemade bread, jams, beets and pickles, and a favorite of both young and old, Church Peanut Butter (peanut butter mixed with marshmallow cream and maple syrup). Meantime the man of the house must transport the benches, hymnals, and dishes to his farm. Most districts have specially designed carriages that hold the church benches. The typical backless benches are made of finely varnished oak, with hinged legs that fold underneath. The benches are carefully stored inside the carriage, sometimes wrapped in carpet to protect them from scratches. The man of the host house will also serve as usher during the worship service.

When the worshipers arrive, the women and young girls are dropped off near the door while the men and boys take care of the horses and buggies. They finally wind up in several groups carrying on small talk of the day. When the service is about to begin, the worshipers enter and follow a prescribed seating arrangement determined by both sex and age. The first to enter are the bishop, two pastors, and deacons. They are followed by the oldest men, the younger men, and finally unmarried boys. The women also enter in single file with the older ladies followed by the younger girls. This traditional order is the same that will be followed when the noon meal is served. Men and women are seated facing each other. Infants are also brought to the service, although they may need to be taken out and fed sometime during the morning. A typical Amish service begins at 9 a.m. and ends at 12 noon. The long service often brings a smile to seasoned Amish when they notice outside visitors straining to remain seated on the hard wooden benches for that long a time.

The Worship Service

For the most part, the Amish worship service is very uninviting to a visitor. That's because it was never intended for visitors. Instead, the Amish worship service is meant only for those within their fellowship. Aside from being conducted entirely in German, the hymns are lengthy, slow, and nearly impossible for anyone to sing who has not been trained in their style. The sermons and prayers are very long and drawn out.

They follow no standard liturgy although they do hold to the same basic format each service.

1. The opening hymn

Several hymns open the service during which time the pastors meet in an adjoining room to decide who will be chosen that day to preach the two-hour sermon. The second hymn sung is always the *Loblied* (also called *Lobgesang* or "O Gott Vater, Wir Loben Dich" or "Oh God, Father, We Do Praise Thee"). With the singing of this hymn they join in worship with their fellow Amish throughout the country. When the preachers return from their meeting, the singing immediately ends and the service continues.

2. Introductory Sermon (*Anfang*)
3. Prayer (usually done kneeling)
4. Reading of the Bible by the Deacon

> O Gott Vater, Wir Loben Dich
> (Loblied)
>
> 1. O God, Father we do praise Thee,
> And glorify Thy goodness,
> That Thou, O Lord, so graciously
> Revealed Thyself anew to us,
> Hast led us thus together, Lord,
> To admonish us through Thy Word
> So grant us Thy grace to do this.
>
> 2. Open mouths of Thy servants, Lord,
> Be of Thy wisdom giving,
> That they may rightly speak Thy Word,
> Which serves to devout living.
> May it profit to Thy glory!
> Make us for this food hungry;
> This desire, we are requesting.
>
> 3. Give our hearts Thy wisdom also,
> On this earth, enlightenment give
> That Thy Word in us may be known,
> That we be truly devout;
> And live our life in righteousness,
> Heeding Thy Word in steadfastness,
> Abiding from deception free.
>
> 4. Lord, only Thine the kingdom is,
> Thine, the Power, the same;
> The congregation does praise Thee,
> Giving thanks unto Thy Name.
> We plead from the depths of our heart
> That Thou this hour with us art,
> Through Jesus Christ, Amen, be.[3]

5. Main sermon

   Preachers often do not use notes during the sermon. The message exhorts the people to remain faithful and true to God's Word. Often references are made to the *Martyr's Mirror* and several Bible stories.

6. Testimonies by other preachers or members
7. Closing remarks by the one who preached the sermon
8. Prayer
9. Benediction
10. Announcement regarding the next service

11. Closing hymn
12. Dismissal–youngest leave first[4]

Because of the length of the service, crackers and cookies for the children are often passed down the benches. When a young Amish girl and boy are "grown up" they refuse the treat. Unlike most other Christian worship services, the Amish worship has no colored windows, organs, candles, crosses, flowers, vestments, liturgy, offering, pulpit or lectern, baptismal font, altar, or choirs. The entire worship service reflects the humility and unity as is shown in the Amish Gelassenheit.

The worship carried on in the Amish congregation is very law oriented. Sermons exhort the listeners to remain true to the traditions, to obey the laws, to keep their lives free from sin, and to refrain from any close relationship with the world. The hymns and prayers likewise focus especially on the life of the Christian. Sadly, the love of God, the sacrifice of Jesus, the assurance of heaven, and the hope and joy found in the comforting Gospel message is rarely emphasized. The men may be asked to remain after the service if there is any business to carry out, such as a fellow member's conduct.

The Singing

Singing plays an important part in the Amish worship, second only to the preaching of the Word. The singing is intended for their people, and therefore takes on an unusual nature of its own. The music is entirely without accompaniment. Instruments are forbidden in worship for they are contrary to the teachings of humility. Many church Ordnung specifically name pianos, organs, violins, and guitars as instruments that are to be avoided. Their claim is that nowhere in the New Testament is there any mention of musical instruments. Instead they insist that Scripture is opposed to them citing Amos 6:1-5 "Woe to you who…strum away on your harps like David and improvise on musical instruments." And 1 Corinthians 14:7 says, "Even in the case of lifeless things that make sounds, such as the flute or harp." There is always the fear that the beautiful sounds of musical instruments will draw the hearer away from the emphasis of the text. Even children are not allowed to play with musical instruments (other than the harmonica). As one Amish man said, "God gave us voices. Then why should we use instruments?"

The *Ausbund* is the hymnbook used by most Amish today. (Some Amish districts use the *Lieder Buch* or *Liedersammlung* which is smaller than the *Ausbund* but contains many of the same songs.) It is the oldest hymnal still being used by any Christian church. The Amish have remained faithful to these hymns for centuries. Many of the songs date back to the beginning of the Anabaptist reformation. Some of the hymns were written by George Blaurock, Felix Manz, Balthasar Hubmeier, Hans Hut, Menno Simons and Peter Reidemann, all famous fathers of the Anabaptist church.

The oldest collection of fifty-three hymns was written by Anabaptists known as the Philippites. Like the Hutterites, the Philippites lived a communal lifestyle. In 1535 a group of about sixty Philippites led by Michael Schneider left Moravia for Germany in search of peace. Instead they were arrested by the Catholics and imprisoned in the dungeons at Passau, a castle in Bavaria on the

---

Selected verses from Ausbund Hymn #36 by Annelein Freiburg who was drowned and later burned in 1529.

1. Everlasting Father in heaven,
I call to you so ardently.
Do not let me turn from you.
Keep me in your truth
Until my final end.

4. To walk through your power into death,
Through sorrow, torture, fear and want,
Sustain me in this,
O God, so that I nevermore
Be separated from your love.

7. They have imprisoned me.
I wait, O God, with all my heart,
With a very great longing,
When finally you will awake
And set your prisoners free.

13. I entrust myself to God and his church.
May he be my protector today,
For the sake of his name.
May this come to pass, Father mine,
Through Jesus Christ. Amen.

Danube River. During the imprisonment the captives spent their time writing long poetic hymns. Many of them were set to the tunes of local folk songs so they could sing them to one another without being singled out. It is suggested that the reason today's hymns are sung so slowly is to reflect the slow singing carried on in prison so the jailers could not dance to the hymns. Although none of the Philippites were executed, they disbanded as soon as they were released from Passau. In 1564 one of the members published a songbook that contained fifty-three of the Passau hymns. Many of the Schneider hymns are favorites of the Amish today, who sing them at special occasions like weddings or when excommunicated members return.[5]

When listening to an Amish hymn, one cannot help but notice the long slow chant-like sounds, similar to the Gregorian chant used by the church throughout the ages. Here again is seen the prayerful, humble ways of Gelassenheit. The *Ausbund* contains no melodies. Instead the melodies are sung just as they were handed down from generation to generation. The melodies are repeated over and over again so that the younger children might remember them. A Mennonite Professor at Goshen College, Indiana, has said, "No one has yet written these tunes in a conventional music score and, even if it were possible to do so, it would be impossible to teach anyone to reproduce their tone and spirit accurately. The Amish sing them with depth and sincerity, a feeling of true Christian piety difficult to imitate. It is literally true that even if anyone would know the tunes, he could not sing them as the Amish do. Anyone wishing to reproduce the tunes must first of all be sincere in trying to know and understand the Amish people. He must understand and feel the context of the words."[6] Harmony is never allowed in their songs, unlike the Hutterites who pride themselves in their beautiful part-singing.

The *Ausbund* contains 140 hymns on over 800 pages of verse. Many of the hymns are long, with up to thirty-seven verses, and may take a half hour to sing (although few hymns are sung in their entirety). It is well known that the more conservative the church district, the slower the hymn singing. In some churches the *Loblied* takes eleven minutes to sing while in others it can take up to twenty minutes.

The hymns are introduced by a specially chosen man called the *Vorsinger* or song leader. This person sets the pitch and sings the first syllable of each line as a solo introducing the hymn to the congregation. He is often chosen because of his expertise in knowing the hymns. At times the *Vorsinger* may ask a younger member to lead the singing.[7] In many Amish communities there is a "practice" hymn sing on the Thursday prior to the worship service for anyone who wishes to learn and practice the songs ahead of time. The Amish also print small "cheater" booklets titled the *Ausbund Lieder Mit Noten* that shows a rough notation of several hymns from the Ausbund. This book is especially helpful to the young Amish who are still learning the hymns.

Amish teens often enjoy singing songs that have "fast tunes". These songs are reserved for their Sunday evening hymn sings, where they get to meet and enjoy fellowship with the youth from several church districts. These songs are still sung in unison and without accompaniment. The hymns are more "Gospel oriented" like "Sweet Hour of Prayer" and "What a Friend We Have in Jesus". Sometimes these hymns might even be sung in English.

The Communion Service and Foot Washing

Communion services are held twice each year, in autumn and spring, as was proposed many years ago by Jacob Ammann. These services are given far greater importance than the regular worship services. Following the teachings of the Amish confessions, communion is celebrated to remember the suffering and death of Christ, but not to receive his true body and blood. Here each member confesses his or her sins and their willingness to serve the Lord and hold fast to the rules of the Ordnung. Prior to the service a congregational meeting is held to review each of the Ordnung rules. Because the communion service is to be a service of peace, the rules must be agreed upon by everyone in the congregation or the service will be delayed. No member should attend this service harboring feelings of hatred. Sometimes members within the district who have been guilty of an offense are excluded from the communion service. This is also an ideal time to receive back into fellowship a straying soul who had been excommunicated but has since repented. Fasting is also done prior to the worship service. Children usually do not attend these services because of the length, and because they are intended especially for the baptized adults. The communion service generally lasts five or six hours and includes a light meal in the middle. The three hours of sermons begin with Genesis and continue through the death of Christ. Near the end of the service, a minister will prepare the bread and wine for the communion celebration. The bread is home-made bread and the wine is often made by the bishop's wife. (Some Amish districts use grape juice instead of wine.)

After the bread and wine have been received the minister retells the story of Jesus washing the feet of the disciples while the deacon readies pails of water and towels. Each of the members removes his or her shoes and stockings as they pair up with a person sitting nearby to wash one another's feet. This is followed by a holy kiss and the words, "The Lord be with us," by one individual, and "Amen, in peace," by the other. They also give a monetary offering to the deacon, the only time of the year that an offering is collected in their worship service.[8]

Choosing Bishops, Ministers, and Deacons

The leadership in each district consists of one bishop or *Voelliger-Diener* ("minister with full powers"), two or three ministers or preachers, who are also called *Diener zum Buch* ("ministers of the book"), and a deacon or *Armen-Diener* ("minister to the poor").[9] The bishop is the leader of the congregation and has included in his responsibilities the administration of communion, baptism, marriages and excommunications. He may also announce other disciplinary action against a wayward member.

The minister's main calling is to preach at Sunday morning worship services. On off Sundays he may visit a nearby district where he will likely be called upon to deliver the main sermon. The minister also assists with the distribution of communion.

Deacons are used for reading the Scripture in the worship service and they see to the needs of the poor and the widowed. In the baptism worship service the deacon assists in the baptismal rite. He is also assigned the distasteful task of notifying the fallen that they are being considered for excommunication. The deacon also serves as the messenger prior to weddings. When a couple wishes to be married the bridegroom informs the deacon of his desires. The deacon will then seek out and ask the bride's parents if they approve of the marriage. If so, he will then tell the bishop, who in turn will announce it in the worship service.

There is no formal training for these men, nor is there any salary or compensation. Ministers are common people who have no experience or training in the operation of a church. This is likely one reason why the Amish churches lack any planned programs like evangelism, stewardship, spiritual growth, budgets, and youth programs. It can happen that one day a young Amish man attends church as a farmer, and returns home as a minister for life (and still a farmer). Never does a young man hint that he would like to be chosen as a minister for that would be presumptuous and a sin of pride. According to the order of things, any married man can be chosen to become a preacher or a deacon. Only ministers may be chosen to serve in the highest office of bishop. Deacons must first move up to the office of minister before becoming a bishop.

All church workers are chosen strictly by lot. On the Sunday of selection, usually a communion Sunday, the members are asked to vacate the worship area while visiting bishops and ministers prepare two booths for voting, one for the women and one for the men. Each member files past the bishop or presiding minister and whispers the name of the candidate of their choice. The recommendations are then tabulated. When the list has been established, the second vote takes place. This narrows the list of candidates. The presiding ministers again tabulate the vote. Each candidate is then asked to leave the room while an equal number of *Ausbund* hymnbooks are prepared. In one of the books there is placed a slip of paper stating "The lot is cast into the lap, but the whole disposing thereof is of the Lord" (Proverbs 16:33). Then the hymnbooks are shuffled and laid across a table. The men are asked to return to the room. The man who received the first vote is the first to pick up a hymnbook and see if it contains the special piece of paper. If it does not, the next man chooses a hymnbook. When one of the men finally finds the special hymnbook, he is asked to step forward to the front of the room. There he will bow down on his knees, and receive blessings from the ministers present. From that moment until his death he has been chosen to lead his people and he cannot refuse the responsibility.

The worship service in which a new minister is chosen often takes on a very somber mood and might even include weeping and sobbing. The people realize the enormous weight of responsibility that is being placed on the newly appointed man. All the members of the congregation are asked to pray for the chosen servant. The choice, they say, has been made by God!

Amish Divisions

One might think that all Amish are alike. That is not necessarily true. Since each district writes its own rules there can be many differences. This is often evident when visiting Amish areas from state to state and even within Amish communities. The four major branches of Amish generally divide among conservative and more liberal.

Old Order Amish

The Old Order is the largest and most traditional of the Amish today. These are the direct descendants of Jacob Ammann and the Swiss Anabaptists. The use of the term Old Order began in the 1860's when about two-thirds of the group split off to form a more liberal branch, the Amish Mennonite Church. Eventually this group joined the mainstream Mennonite Church. The remaining third took on the name Old Order as a distinguishing title. Today the Old Order makes up about 85% of all Amish.

AMISH GROUPS
Old Order Amish 1250 districts 190,000 people
New Order Amish 75 districts 9000 people
Beachy Amish 100 districts 14,000 people
Amish Mennonites 30 districts 4000 people

Within the Old Order Amish are several subgroups, each with different characteristics. The Swiss Amish of Indiana speak a Swiss dialect. The Byler group uses yellow buggies. The Renno group asks their men to wear only one suspender. The Nebraska Amish are known for their white-topped buggies. The most conservative Old Order group is the Schwartzentruber Amish.[10]

New Order Amish

The New Order Amish, sometimes called the Amish Brotherhood, began in Ohio in the 1960's. They allow Bible studies for the youth, emphasize a more personal salvation (as opposed to the community philosophy of the Old Order), and are more flexible in their approach to technology, allowing telephones and electricity. Some New Order churches have Sunday school classes and church outreach programs.

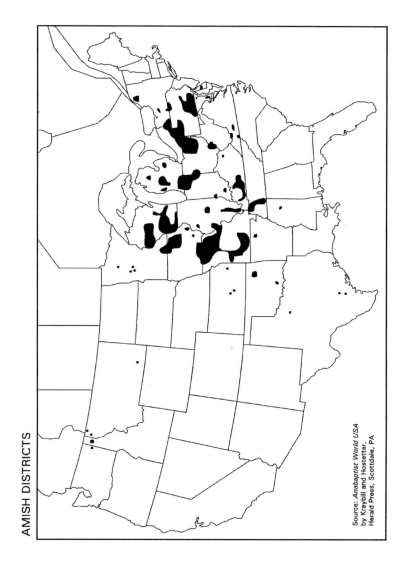

Beachy Amish

Some Amish groups derived their name from a particular early leader. The Beachy Amish of Pennsylvania is such a group. They began in the 1920's when a problem arose in a Pennsylvania Amish church over shunning. Some members of the church joined a more liberal Amish Mennonite church just over the Maryland border. Because the two congregations were once a single church, there were many family ties and friendships that had been established. However the strict Amish bishop, Moses Yoder, followed the letter of the law and excommunicated and shunned all those who left for the Maryland church. This practice continued until a new bishop, Moses Beachy, joined the Pennsylvania church in 1916. He believed it was not wise to shun those who had left. Consequently there was a division in 1927. Beachy's group was the more liberal. Within one year Beachy's congregation began a Sunday school and his members lit up their homes with electricity. Automobile ownership, relaxed dress standards, and a church building soon followed.

Amish Mennonites

As mentioned previously, in the 1960's two-thirds of the Amish formed the Amish Mennonite church, which later merged into the Mennonite group. Among these Amish there were still a handful of congregations that welcomed the Mennonite heritage, yet still wished to keep their Amish identity. Today this small group is called the Amish Mennonites. Their lifestyle is very similar to the Beachy Amish. While driving the back roads, if you ever spot a church with a sign above the door saying AMISH, it is likely an Amish Mennonite church.

The Amish church is estimated to be doubling in numbers every twenty years. States with the largest Amish population beginning with the greatest number are Ohio, Pennsylvania, Indiana, Wisconsin, and Michigan.

1. Donald B. Kraybill, *The Riddle of the Amish*, p. 14.
2. Joe Wittmer, *The Gentle People*, p. 96.
3. *Hymn Translations, German to English*, p. 61.
4. John A. Hostetler, *Amish Society*, p. 213.
5. Brad Igou, *The Amish in Their Own Words*, p. 182.
6. Brad Igou, *The Amish in Their Own Words*, p. 184.
7. Joe Wittmer, *The Gentle People*, p. 98.
8. Donald B. Kraybill, *Anabaptist World USA*, p. 68.
9. John A. Hostetler, *Amish Society*, p. 106.
10. Donald B. Kraybill, *On the Backroad to Heaven*, p. 109.
11. Donald B. Kraybill, *Anabaptist World USA*, p. 68.

CHAPTER 7
Within the Amish Community

While driving the back roads of Amish country, one notices many scenes repeated over and over again. White houses, beautifully weeded gardens, windows covered with dark curtains, buggies parked somewhere in the gravel driveways, all signs that you are deep within Amish country. But there is something missing in that picture. People!

Young and old people may not appear in that picture because they are busy with their daily chores and duties. You may not see the small children in the henhouse gathering eggs, the young lads busy in the barn feeding the cows, or the young ladies laundering their clothes in the wringer washer. The Amish home is very alive. To these people, the home and the church community are the two most precious things they know, and they are certain to take good care of both.

Birth

"Put a swing where the children want it. The grass will grow back." That old Amish saying has been repeated many times. Children play an important role in Amish culture. Amish couples never practice birth control, but instead they pray for children because they believe the Bible tells them to increase and multiply. As a result it is common for an Amish family to have at least six children and often more. With that number of children born to Amish families, it is not unusual for a youngster to have between fifty and one hundred first cousins, all living within a few miles. Author Joe Witmer wrote in his book *The Gentle People: Personal Reflections of Amish Life*: "A baby means another corn-husker, another cow-milker, but, most of all, another God-fearing Amishman. The birth is always seen as a blessing from the Lord. Thus, Amish parents feel that their children really do not belong to them."[1]

One Amish mother put it this way, "If these were MY children, I would love them so much I couldn't bear to punish them. But because they are from the Lord, I will punish them when necessary...If these were MY children I would want to dress them attractively to draw attention to the natural beauty which God has blessed them with. However, because they are God's children I will dress them modestly so they will not be strangers to God's dress...If these were MY children I would want to send them to the best schools, have them read all the current best sellers, and in every way fit them to obtain good jobs, and live a life of ease. But since these are God's children, I will send them to a Christian day school to help fit them for eternity, and trust God to lead them when school years are past....If these were MY children as they enter their teen years, I would provide them with all the "extras," a car, radio, television and the latest fashionable clothes. But since these are God's children, I will admonish them and try to impress upon them that 'what a man sows, that must he also reap.' If these were MY children and I followed my own selfish desires I would share with them as much as possible in enjoying the worldly pleasures. I would also spend with them an endless eternity in the torments of hell and I would be largely responsible as their mother for influencing them in that direction."[2]

Most Amish children are born at home with the help of family members and a mid-wife, although they are not against using a hospital if necessary. The birth is a very precious moment, yet it is also viewed as a somewhat uneventful moment.

The extended family of relatives and friends express their joy over the new birth, but again it is seen as just a natural happening within their relation. The newborn will likely sleep in the parents' bedroom and is always found in the arms of a family member. The Amish do not have such things as baby showers. The infant simply becomes a part of the loving Amish home that is structured in such a way that the children have their definite place as do the parents. As the children grow older, discipline, including spanking, becomes necessary in order to break the ego and teach obedience, humility, respect, and modesty. Amish parents are careful not to teach their youngsters English for at least the first several years. They want their children to get to know and hear the German language as the primary language spoken in their Amish house.

An Amish home is one of constant education. Girls learn the art of maintaining an organized household and the young boys discover the knowledge and work ethic that goes with operating a successful farm or business. Parents are careful to set good examples for their families. Loud and boisterous arguments between adults or with children are a rarity. Amish families would much prefer that both parents remain at home as they raise their families. There they are able to interact with one another throughout the day, including enjoying three meals together. However, Amish society does not always allow that, and there are many "lunch pail" Amish fathers who must go into town to earn a paycheck.

Education

Education plays another very important role in the raising of Amish children. Much negative commentary has condemned the Amish for neglecting their children's education simply because they do not allow their children to continue in school beyond eighth grade. But the truth is really quite different. Amish children are constantly learning the necessities of life from their parents and elders in the community. It could almost be said that Amish youngsters are better equipped in the art of living than are their English counterparts. The goal of education in Amish society is only to serve the Amish church and Amish family. Beyond that, education is deemed harmful.

Today the Amish operate nearly 1200 schools for 32,000 children.[3] Amish children attend school through eighth grade. They believe that by then the children have had ample opportunity to learn the basics of education, including the English language. High schools, they feel, are designed to teach worldly children to serve themselves, to become independent, to achieve social recognition and self-improvement. These are all contrary to the philosophy of Gelassenheit. Over the years the eighth grade policy has caused many problems in state districts where Amish parents have been taken to court and even jailed for their educational beliefs. In 1972 the subject came to a head as the case of *Wisconsin vs. Yoder* went to the United States Supreme Court. The state of Wisconsin demanded that the children continue their education beyond elementary school years. The Supreme Court ruled in favor of the Amish, stating that their education did not end after eighth grade. It merely continued in a different form.

> WISCONSIN vs. YODER
> 1972 SUPREME COURT RULING:
> "There can be no assumption that today's majority is 'right' and the Amish and others are 'wrong.' A way of life that is odd or even erratic but interferes with no rights or interests of others is not to be condemned because it is different."[4]

Throughout the early and middle part of the 1900's, most Amish attended one room public schools established to serve the rural communities. By the late 1950's many of these schools consolidated into larger schools, and they began to teach some subjects that were "questionable" to the Amish community, such as evolution and sex education. As a result many of the Amish communities purchased the abandoned one room school buildings and remodeled them for their own use.

Most of these classroom buildings are without electricity or indoor plumbing. Outside the school building is a white outhouse and a shed for protecting wood for the wood stove. Many school buildings have two doors at the school entrance—one for girls and one for boys. A typical school would include wooden desks of various sizes, chalkboard, pegs for straw hats and coats, and even a pot-bellied stove and rope-pulled bell. Many classrooms also have extra benches lining the back walls called "visitor benches" for parents, school board members and others in the community who would like to sit in on a typical school day. Playgrounds are modestly equipped with swing sets, teeter-totters, and perhaps a ball diamond.

Amish teachers are usually young unmarried ladies, at least age seventeen, who themselves graduated with an eighth grade education. Most states do not require that they be certified. Teachers receive a daily salary for their work. They teach and supervise sometimes as many as thirty children in grades 1-8. The teacher holds scheduled meetings with both parents and a school board that is elected to oversee the entire program. Although there is no centralized headquarters and no school principal to assist these teachers, they do have opportunity to share ideas and concerns with other Amish teachers at specially scheduled meetings and through an Amish publication by Amish publisher Pathway Press called the *Blackboard Bulletin.*

Class subjects include phonics and reading, spelling, English, grammar, German, penmanship, mathematics, history, and geography. Although health is a regular subject, science is often not a part of the curriculum. Some schools also offer classes in agriculture. Textbooks are outdated, very basic and void of much color. Students are discouraged from becoming overly interested in one subject like animals, astronomy, or the Civil War. Students are also not permitted to use a public library or collect books for themselves. They are allowed to read simple classics like *Black Beauty*, but mysteries and romance novels are forbidden.

The school day begins with prayer and Bible reading, and all subjects are taught in the light of God's Word, however ironically, religion is not taught as an academic subject. The Amish believe that religious teaching should be reserved for the home and the church.

Grading is strict and grading on a curve is not acceptable. The Amish are concerned that extra time be spent with those who need remedial help. Some Amish schools today even hire additional help for special education.

The school day begins about 8:30 a.m. and ends at 3:30 p.m., like most other schools. The day includes an opening devotion with the Lord's Prayer, recitations, spelling bees, skits and of course the three R's. Lunch hour includes a sack lunch. In winter children often bring soup or dinner leftovers to be heated atop the stove. Like other children, Amish youngsters wait impatiently for their chance to go outside and play. Recess provides young and old barefooted Amish children an opportunity to play a variety of games in the school yard. Children get very few school holidays. School boards would much rather set up a yearly schedule that would get in the required 180 days as quickly as possible so the children can help with the spring planting.

Ever since the Amish began overseeing their own schools, there has been a need for more parent involvement. Local school boards of four or five fathers are responsible for hiring the teacher, approving the school curriculum, maintaining the building and setting the school budget. In many Amish schools, parents must sign their names in agreement with the school rules and disciplines.

In some districts parents are assessed a special tax based on their property values. Other districts follow a "give according to what you can afford" system.

Amish schools are designed to prepare Amish children to be God-fearing and hard working individuals. They teach their children the necessary basics to function as members of the Amish community, the home, and the larger "worldly society", always teaching the virtues of humility, selflessness, and personal responsibility. Many businesses located within Amish communities seek to employ young Amish men and women because they know that these teens can be trusted to give an honest day's work for an honest day's pay.

Rumspringa

As in many cultures, the teen years are often the most difficult. The Amish community is not immune from the problems that restless teens experience as they desperately try to find their identity. In Amish society the "adolescent years" are between their formal home training and becoming an accepted member of the Amish church through the rite of baptism. However, beginning at about age sixteen they experience a period of wandering called Rumspringa ("running around") or "sowing wild oats." This is a time when Amish youth are permitted to find their Amish friends. These Amish cliques are known as gangs. Gangs are typically made up of 50 to 150 young people. Each gang has a name such as the Chickadees or the Cardinals. They are usually made up of both girls and boys, and often have reputations of being a wild gang or a tame gang. This might include anything from wearing "English" clothes, sprucing up the buggy, listening to the radio, going to movies, smoking cigarettes, driving or buying a car, and experimenting with alcohol or even drugs. Many Amish parents go through a painful period as they watch their children experiment with the very things they have been preaching and teaching their children to avoid since they were born. Yet they feel it is a necessary process they must go through because this is the age the youth must begin to make up their minds if they will remain Amish or leave the community.

For the vast majority of Amish youth, Rumspringa is followed by the Amish teenagers making the baptismal promise never to flirt with the world again. If they leave the church prior to their baptism they will not be banned. If they decide to be baptized and then return to the world, they will be both excommunicated and shunned. Surprisingly, an amazing 80-90% of the young people eventually decide to become baptized members. This is certainly a result of their close-knit homes, their many Amish friendships, and their family-like ties with their church district. Moreover these young people have been indoctrinated from little on about the dangers that lie in the world around them. Although Rumspringa sounds like a wild time for Amish teens, far less importance is placed on it by the Amish than by the outside world, where local news media relish the opportunity of headlining articles about young Amish teens getting into trouble with the law. In a very real way, Rumspringa results in a more solid and faithful church member. Each Amish adult realizes he or she once had an opportunity to see the world and they made a resolute decision to remain with the church.

Courtship and Dating

Rumspringa means far more to the Amish teen than just running around. It is also a sign that he or she is ready to begin dating. Age sixteen is the usual age when dating begins. Although it seems that Amish parents simply let go of their children during these years, this is not the case. There are many activities that church districts make available to their teens to keep them in the community. The most popular meeting time is on Sunday evenings when the youth enjoy their "sings." This fellowship opportunity allows young people from several church districts to get together. Often the farm where this takes place is the same one that sponsored the morning worship service. Young men and women make sure they are neat and well groomed with horse and buggy cleaned and in tip-top shape. If a young man plans to escort a young lady home, the lad may even decorate the buggy with fancy bells and bangles. At the sing the young people sit across from one another and sing upbeat Gospel songs. Usually the mother of the house will prepare a tasty meal before the singing begins. The friendships formed here often last a lifetime.

Other youth gatherings may include skating parties, volleyball nights or taffy pulls, each giving them the opportunity to socialize with the opposite sex. Contrary to some beliefs, Amish marriages are not arranged. The Amish marry for love, although parent acceptance of the boy or girl is very important.

> **THE FIRST DATE**
> A young couple's first date together may be rather stressful. Often they are followed by a wagon full of "cut-ups", other boyfriends and girlfriends who follow them to her house. They will continually harass the young couple, and if the opportunity arises, they will remove the wheels from his buggy or turn his horse loose. "I remember one particular incident in which the 'cut-ups' worked very hard taking a young man's buggy apart and rebuilt it straddle of the barn's roof peak—40 feet up."[5]

Dating begins when a young man invites a young lady home in his buggy. Secrecy is important while dating. Although close friends and relatives are aware of the courtship, it is not disclosed openly. Couples who are going steady will often meet on a Saturday night. Seldom will they ever spend time together in the daylight. The young man may call on his girlfriend after the "old folks" have gone to bed. He might shine a light on her window. The night is spent playing games and enjoying each other's company. If they are truly serious with each other, they may spend much of the time discussing their upcoming wedding or her dowry, which has been accumulating over the years. A typical dowry will include silverware, quilts and other useful items for the home.[6] Sexual contact is strongly condemned among the Amish, and illegitimate births are rare. If a young couple is caught having sex, they must confess before the church and are shunned for an amount of time. If the young lady becomes pregnant it is understood that she will marry the young man. Years ago the young dating Amish spent their nights lying on a bed fully clothed. This practice called "bundling" followed an old custom dating back to the time when there was little heat in the homes. Today bundling has either disappeared or it is strongly discouraged.

A young man may marry a young girl from another community, but she must be Amish and they both must be baptized prior to their marriage. (Choosing an Amish mate from another settlement could cause problems if the settlements are not in total agreement with one another. Amish are even leery of accepting fellow Amish into their midst.) Selecting a spouse is an important process since divorce is never allowed and is grounds for excommunication and shunning. First cousin marriages are not permitted and second cousin marriages are discouraged due to serious health problems that have arisen over the years.

Baptism

The most distinguishing mark of the Anabaptist movement is their view that only adults are capable of devoting their lives to the Lord through the rite of baptism. The Amish believe that infants do not need to be baptized because they claim that Christ's suffering and death was sufficient to atone for the sins of the children. Only the adult who has undergone thorough instruction may be baptized–usually between the ages of sixteen and twenty-two. Baptism must occur before marriage, and once a young Amish man or lady becomes baptized, there is no turning back.

Following the spring communion service classes are held for the young people who wish to be baptized. They meet with the ministers on worship Sundays where they are instructed in the articles of the Dordrecht Confession. This instruction lasts until August when a date is set for the baptism worship service, to be held just before the fall communion service. A week prior to the baptism, the minister meets with the applicants and stresses the need to walk the "straight and narrow" after their baptism. At this meeting students are also given one last opportunity to turn back if they are uncertain of their desires. Young men are also told that their baptism promise includes their willingness to serve as minister if ever chosen to do so, and the young ladies are told they must support their husbands if they are called upon to serve the church. Prior to the baptism service the congregation is given the opportunity to voice its approval or disapproval of the class about to be baptized.

The baptism worship service begins when the young people take their places in the front of the congregation. They sit quietly with heads bowed and hands over their faces, signifying their willingness to submit to the authority of God and the church. The deacon provides a small pail of water and a cup. He tells the young people to kneel "before the Most High God and His Church." The deacon then pours water into the hands of the bishop who lets the water drip down the heads of the baptized. He then says, "May the Lord God complete the good work which he has begun in you and strengthen and comfort you to a blessed end through Jesus Christ. Amen." This is then followed with a "holy kiss" by the bishop for each of the young men,

---

THE BAPTISMAL VOW

1. As the Ethiopian eunuch confessed, can you confess, "Yes, I believe that Jesus Christ is the Son of God?"
Answer: Yes.

2. Do you confess this to be a Christian order, church and congregation of God to which you now submit?
Answer: Yes

3. Do you also denounce the world, the devil, with all his doings, as well as your own flesh and blood and do you desire to live only for Jesus Christ who died for you on the cross and who arose again?
Answer: Yes

4. Do you promise before God and the congregation that this order you will help manage, help counsel and labor in this congregation and never swerve with God's help, if it results either to life or to death?
Answer: Yes [7]

and by the bishop's wife for each of the young ladies. Soon the new members are in full fellowship with the rest of the congregation, and able to enjoy all the rights of their fellow baptized members.[8] Now they are truly Amish!

Weddings

As with all other rites and ceremonies in the Amish society, marriage also follows a strict and orderly process. Once again the rules and ordinances dictate when, how and to whom a marriage will take place, for only by stringent control can the colony of believers remain intact. A couple is engaged when a young man asks his beloved to marry him. Since jewelry is not permitted, there will be no engagement ring, although he may impress her with a gift of a fancy household item. Although families know what is about to take place, they hide their feelings until the plans are formally announced in July or August. One can usually sense there will be a wedding in the family if an unusually large garden is planted in the spring.[9]

The engagement takes place when a young man secretly sends a close friend to the bride's home to meet with her parents and ask for her hand. Once the parents have consented to the marriage, the ministers meet privately with both the bride and groom for counseling. Following the fall communion service, the engaged couples are "published" or *Ausgerufen* by the deacon or bishop. On that Sunday the couple is excused from worship so the young man may go over to his fiancées house for a special dinner she has prepared. Early winter weddings are

---

WEDDING CELERY
A good sign of an impending wedding is an unusual amount of celery planted in early spring. Celery plays an important part in weddings. (Some times the neighbors help out by also planting some extra just in case.) Some of the celery is used in an Amish casserole–often part of the main course. The celery is part of the bread stuffing for the chicken. More celery is used to make creamed celery, a standard side dish. The final use is...instead of flowers, most Amish wedding dinner tables are decorated with vases and jars filled with stalks of celery.

popular because work in the fields has finished by then. Weddings are scheduled on a Tuesday or Thursday because Mondays, Wednesdays, and Fridays are reserved for preparations and cleanup. Saturday weddings would not work because it would be sacrilegious to clean up on a Sunday. As many as a dozen weddings may take place on the same day within the settlement. The wedding always takes place in the young lady's home and may include up to 400 guests. Much time and hard work go into preparing for the wedding. Barns need to be cleaned, sheds need new paint, and the house must be cleaned from top to bottom. Some Amish even whitewash the trunks of trees around the house to give them a fresh clean look. The bridegroom is responsible to send out all invitations, either by personal contact or by mail.

> **THE MARRIAGE VOWS**
>
> Do you acknowledge and confess it as a Christian order that there should be one husband and one wife, and are you able to have the confidence that you have begun this undertaking in accordance with the way you have been taught? (Yes)
>
> Do you also have the confidence, brother, that the Lord has ordained this, our fellow sister, as a marriage partner for you? (Yes)
>
> Do you also have the confidence, sister, that the Lord has ordained this, our fellow brother, as a marriage partner for you? (Yes)
>
> Do you solemnly promise your wife that if she should be afflicted with bodily weakness, sickness, or some such similar circumstance, that you will care for her as is fitting for a Christian husband? (Yes)
>
> And do you promise the same to your husband, that if he should be afflicted with bodily weakness, sickness, or some such similar circumstance, that you will care for him as is fitting for a Christian wife? (Yes)
>
> And do you both solemnly promise each other that you will love and be patient with each other and not separate from each other until God shall separate you through death? (Yes)[10]

The wedding day begins about 4:00 a.m. with the usual milking chores. Aunts and uncles arrive by 6:30 a.m. to help with the dinner details. They had likely been there several days earlier to help begin meal preparations. One recollection of an Amish wedding listed seven borrowed or rented gas stoves that were moved into the kitchen plus seven camping stoves and seventeen roasters to help prepare the chicken and other hot foods. Six to seven hundred pounds of ice were unloaded into the icehouse to refrigerate the 300 pounds of chicken.[11] The noon meal consists of chicken with bread filling, mashed potatoes, gravy, creamed celery, cabbage, and plenty of rich pies, puddings and cakes for dessert, plus the bride and groom will likely have a wedding cake.[12] Guests may also bring snacks and candy for the special *Eck* or corner table where the bride and groom are seated. (The young man sits on the right and the young lady at his left–the same way they will sit in their buggy.) There will be several sittings because of the number of people attending.

The worship service begins at 8:30 or 9:00 a.m. It is a typical three hour service, with prayers, singing, two sermons and testimonials by leaders and relatives. The sermons and Bible readings relate to the marriage taking place. Sometimes the book of *Tobit* is read during the marriage service. (*Tobit* is one of the books of the Apocrypha, books that are not considered by Protestant churches to be part of the inspired canonical books. The Amish agree that these books are good and beneficial to read, but are not part of the Holy Bible.) The *Forgeher* or ushers help seat everyone attending the service. Often the service is held in the same rooms that will be needed later for the huge dinner meal. The bride and groom meet upstairs with the bishop and deacons during the singing of the first few hymns where they receive some important last minute counseling on the responsibilities in a Christian marriage. The bishop marries the couple after they recite their wedding vows. The service is stripped of all wedding adornments that would be found at most "worldly" weddings. There are no flowers, no organ playing or soloist, no fancy wedding dress, no lace, no candles, no photographs (pictures may be taken of the decorated room and cake, but none showing any people), and of course no rings. The bride is dressed in a new dark blue plain-cut dress, the same style she wears to Sunday worship services. She will also wear a black prayer covering in place of a veil. The bride's apron and shawl will be safely kept because it will likely be worn when she is buried. She does choose a few attendants or *Newehockers* ("sidesitters") to assist her. There is no maid of honor or best man because that would set them apart from the others.

The groom is dressed in his finest black hat and black suit fastened with hooks and eyes. He and his *Newehocker* attendants wear white shirts, black socks and shoes, and perhaps for this special occasion–a black bow tie.[13]

After the service the festivities begin with a fabulous dinner. Tables are arranged in a "U" shape and the bridesmaids seat the guests. (If someone attends who has been shunned, they will be given a table in a corner of the room away from the other guests.)

The afternoon is spent with games for the younger children and plenty of fellowship for the adults. Sometimes the bride and groom pair up all the single young men and women, telling them to spend the rest of the day together as a couple. By 10 p.m. the day has been well spent for there will be cleaning and chores early in the morning. The bride and groom spend their first night in the house of the bride's parents. Their honeymoon is spent visiting friends and relatives for the next several weekends. This is when they receive most of their wedding gifts, which include practical items for the home or the shop. The couple continues to live with the bride's family until they can set up housekeeping on their own. Once married, the wife no longer wears the white cape and white aprons to church services. Rather, she now wears aprons, capes and bonnets that match the dark color of her dress. The young groom begins to grow a beard, signifying that he is a married man.

Men usually marry between the ages of eighteen and twenty-two, and women slightly younger. Those women who do not marry stop attending the singings in their early twenties and often help with child-rearing duties in their homes. Sometimes they will seek employment in the community as waitresses or store clerks. They will often be chosen to marry older Amish widowers. Remarriage is encouraged about two years after one's spouse has died.

The Grandpa House

When driving the back roads, one can't help but notice the interesting configurations of the Amish houses. Attached to many of the main house frames or built near the main house, will be another house that seems to have been added at a later time. This is the *Dawdy Haus* or "grandpa house." To the Amish, keeping families together is very important. Young Amish couples would never allow their aged parents to live alone or to be housed in an "old age facility". Instead, they see to it when the time comes that an extra addition is added to the house for their parents or grandparents. Some Amish homes have several additions attached. The *Dawdy Haus* is small, yet very accommodating.

The common age of retirement is about fifty. That's not to say that the older folks are cut off from work. They are given an option to work full-time or not at all. If their health is good, they may put in full days of work for many more years. Retired husbands and wives spend more time with their relatives and friends. They still enjoy the fellowship of weddings, auctions, and frolics as they did when younger. The older they become, the more respect they command within the community. If they become ill, many friends and relatives stop in to visit. To the Amish, aging is a natural progression in life. Each day is lived the same, whether it includes a major celebration or simply another day of chores.

1. Joe Wittmer, *The Gentle People: Personal Reflections of Amish Life*, p. 60.
2. Ibid. p. 61,62.
3. Donald B. Kraybill, *On the Backroad to Heaven*, p. 114.
4. Donald B. Kraybill, *The Riddle of the Amish Culture*, p. 162.
5. Joe Wittmer, *The Gentle People: Personal Reflections of Amish Life*, p. 123.
6. John A. Hostetler, *Amish Society*, p. 148.
7. Brad Igou, *The Amish in Their Own Words*, p. 190.
8. Donald B. Kraybill, *The Riddle of the Amish Culture*, p. 119.
9. Joe Wittmer, *The Gentle People: Personal Reflections of Amish Life*, p. 130
10. Brad Igou, *The Amish in Their Own Words*, p. 96.
11. www.amish-heartland.com.
12. Donald B. Kraybill, *On the Backroad to Heaven*, p. 121.
13. http://www.800padutch.com/amish.shtml

CHAPTER 8
Amish Traditions

Traveling the back roads of the Amish countryside one cannot help but notice that every Amish home has a clothesline weighed down with pants and shirts. Monday is usually wash day, and there is a silent competition among Amish women to see who can get their wet laundry pinned to the clothesline first. Hung in distinctive order, from longest pants to the shortest, one gets a feel for the style clothing that this society takes very seriously. After all, just like everything else in the Amish customs, the clothing is a direct reflection of their religion. They never decided to wear the clothes they do to make them look odd to those around them. Quite the opposite, in the early years of the Anabaptist movement they chose clothing that would keep them from standing out among the rest of the peasants.

Dress

Today's department store racks are filled with the latest fashions. Fads come and go, and new styles are constantly advertised. Society is intent on marketing whatever will satisfy people's craving to look smart, keep up with the latest, appear stylish, and cause those around to take notice. Twenty-first century clothing is designed to set the individual apart from the rest. After all, doesn't everyone enjoy being complimented on their latest wardrobe?

Not everyone. The Amish community dresses for the exact opposite reasons. Instead of trying to set themselves apart from the crowd, their goal is to blend in with the crowd. Instead of stressing individualism and taking pride in social status, the Amish would rather appear equal with everyone else in their community. Self-adornment is a sin. Gelassenheit will simply not allow any form of personal glorification through clothing. As one Amish writer put it, "God designs clothes to cover the body, not display it."[1] From the time they are little children until they die, the Amish wear their clothing to symbolize that they have submitted their will to a higher authority. To them their dress is simply a way of life, a reflection of their faith.

Style and form of dress are not mentioned in either the Schleitheim Articles or the Dordrecht Confession (perhaps because in those days distinctive dress was not an issue), it is nevertheless an important part of every Ordnung. Although there have been minor changes, the dress of the Amish today closely resembles the common clothes worn in the sixteenth and seventeenth centuries. The dress code also defines the individual's age, sex and social position. Special clothing is designed for the young, the unmarried, the married, and there is never a crossover in styles between men and women. Each has its own distinct wardrobe.

This is not to say that every Amish district wears the exact same style clothing. The more conservative Amish districts follow different styles than do the more liberal. A good example is the black hat worn by the men. A wide hat brim, low crown, and narrow hat band is a sign of a more conservative Amish church district. Although the average non-Amish person would never be able to recognize these differences, the Amish can readily spot even the smallest variation at a glance. Amish adults usually have three separate wardrobes, one for church, one for dress-up and one for daily work.

Children's Clothes

Baby girls usually make their appearance in church at about six weeks. They wear a small head covering until about age four when they begin to wear the common white bonnet. Also at age four they begin to wear their hair twisted into rolls and arranged in a bun. Little girls wear dresses that button in the back. They never wear slacks. For dress-up, they may wear a black *Schatzli* or apron. Church dresses are always a solid color. This is standard dress until they reach the teen years and begin to wear a black covering. Amish girls usually wear braided hair, which is fastened together in the back of the head.[2]

For the first year, baby boys often wear baby bonnets, and dresses for easy diaper changing. After that they may change into pants with a button-holed waist that attaches to buttons sewn onto their shirts. At four years, boys begin to wear adult-like suits with vest, suspenders, coat, hat, and "broadfall" trousers with a trapdoor in the front. Boys' (and men's) hair is trimmed with a straight cut at a length that comes about midway down the ear and with straight cut bangs that reach midway down the forehead. The males do not part their hair.

Women's Wardrobe

The *Kapp* or head covering of Amish ladies is a very distinctive part of their dress. The head must be covered twenty-four hours each day (scarves are allowed for outside wear.) Amish believe that the woman's head must be covered in order for her prayers to be heard. They want to be prepared should they awaken in the middle of the night and begin to pray. As with other parts of clothing, this too varies in style from settlement to settlement. Although an outsider would be hard-pressed to notice the subtle differences, the Amish can immediately identify the area and type of Amish simply by the head coverings. The way the hats are sewn, including the fancy pleating, is very specific, and requires a great deal of intricate detail.

The Amish woman's dress is somewhat more colorful than their male counterparts. In some Amish communities, women may wear solid color one-piece dresses without any print pattern. The length of the dress comes midway between the knee and the shoe–usually about eight inches from the floor. Often they will cover the dress with a *Halsduch* or cape. The cape is usually worn to church and for dress up and not as daily wear. After age forty, all women wear a black cape to church. This triangular piece of cloth is brought around the neck and tied together in the lower front. It is usually worn over the apron, which is standard wear around the house. A belt sewn at the top of the apron goes around the waist and is fastened with pins. Young girls begin wearing the apron at about eight years.[3]

Stockings are worn by all females. Baby girls wear white stockings until they are two, when they begin wearing the traditional black stockings. Black tie shoes are necessary for church. Younger women often wear tennis shoes or go barefoot for their daily chores.

In winter women wear woolen shawls or overcoats with a quilted lining. The coat is always black and is fastened with buttons or snaps.

Women in mourning wear black capes and aprons for specified periods of time after the loved one has died. For a spouse, parent, child, brother or sister, they wear this garb for one year. For grandparents or grandchildren they will wear it for six months, three months for aunts, uncles, nieces and nephews, and six weeks for cousins. This symbolic dress is a way of allowing the community to share their grief.[4]

Clothing for Men

As with Amish women, the hat is perhaps the most distinguishing characteristic of the Amish man's wardrobe. Men and boys are to wear their hat whenever they go outdoors. Straw hats are worn for the summer months, and black woolen hats in cooler weather. (The black hats typically sell for about $70.) Hats are usually purchased from Amish hat makers. Boys, older men, and ministers wear a black hat with a smooth crown. Most other men and older boys wear a "telescope" hat that has a crease running around the top rim of the hat. One Amish hat manufacturer provides men's hats with the brim sizes of 2½", 2¾", 3", 3¼", 3½" and 4", to satisfy the Ordnung rules from many different church districts.

> **HARD HAT REGULATIONS**
> In the 1970s the federal government required all those working at a construction site to wear a hard hat. Since this included several Amish laborers in Pennsylvania, the Amish became concerned for the loss of their hats.
>
> Pleading their case to the Secretary of Labor and Industry, they explained that their dress was part of their religious conviction. One witness at the hearing claims that an Amish black hat was passed around the room. When it reached the Secretary he remarked that the hat seemed hard enough to him. The Amish were granted an exemption from the regulation.[5]

Men can wear sunglasses, gloves, and scarves according to the weather. Wristwatches and other jewelry are never allowed for either Amish men or women.

After the Amish broke with the Mennonite Church in the 1600's, the Amish were given the nickname the "hook-and-eyers" (no buttons allowed). The Mennonites, on the other hand, became known as the "button-people". This may have referred to the fact that buttons were just becoming popular with the styles of the wealthy Europeans and the Amish wanted no connection with such trends. Today the Amish do wear buttons on their clothing, although they continue to also use the hook and eye. Buttons are used on men's shirts, trousers, and underwear.

Men's coats and vests are usually fastened with the hook and eye.

Amish men still wear broadfall trousers that have a trap door flap fastened in the front with buttons. These pants are held up with suspenders. Even suspender styles are dictated by the Ordnung, whether the back straps form an "X", "Y", or "H" shape. Shirts are always light colored and seldom include a pocket. For church, the man wears a vest and a special coat called a *Mutze*. This coat has no lapels but is split in the lower back. In warmer weather, Amish men need not wear coats, but continue to wear the vests. Men wear black shoes for church and brown work shoes for daily chores.[6]

Young Amish men remain clean-shaven until they get married. Married men wear beards but no mustaches. It is said that mustaches are forbidden because the soldiers who persecuted the early Anabaptists had mustaches.

As with so many other regulations in Amish life, clothing also presents its share of problems. Although the church is clear in its rules and orders regarding dress, there are always those who try to stretch those rules. Consequently, church officials must deal with the teens who try to "dress around" or bend the rules as far as possible.[7] Some girls wear head coverings far too small for their rules of modesty, often leaving them untied. Likewise dress length can also become a problem, especially with the young girls who must work in local restaurants and stores. Boys who go hatless or try to wear hats with far too small a brim also cause grief to parents and church districts as does length of hair, which they either let grow too long or cut too short.

Sewing and Quilting

The Amish woman is responsible for her family's clothing and spends many hours sewing shirts, pants, and dresses. Considering the size of the normal Amish family, this is quite a task even though undergarments, gloves, and socks can be bought at a local Amish dry goods store. Corduroy and prints are not allowed, however, in recent years, polyester materials have been permitted in some Amish districts. The sewing is done on a treadle-operated sewing machine–often in the summer months so the children will be ready for school in the fall.

> The average quilt requires 250-350 yards of thread. Some Amish women have used more than 1000 yards or more of thread on a single quilt. The record is held by the Shetlers of Kentucky who once used 1270 yards of thread.[8]

An obvious sign of Amish identity and tradition is the quilt. Known worldwide for their quality and beauty, Amish quilts often demand a price of $1000 or more. It is not unusual for a fine quilt to take up to a year to complete. Today many Amish families and church districts rely on the income generated by their quilts. The Amish did not invent the quilt. They were crafted many years before the Anabaptists began. It wasn't until the late 1800's that Amish women began to concentrate on this form of folk art. Now an important part of the Amish home, Amish girls are taught the art, and Amish women appreciate the social outlet it brings to their lives. Quilt making is usually a winter project. Ironically, most Amish quilts are not allowed to be used in Amish homes because of their bright colors.

Diet

The Amish are hearty eaters! Thus, the Amish diet is one of sweet indulgence, often resulting in weight problems in later life. Meat and potatoes are a mainstay in the Amish home. Amish women spend much of their time at the stove cooking up a favorite meal or canning foods they will need throughout the winter months. Fresh vegetables and fruits are always welcome by the family during growing season. Amish keep immaculate gardens that are always well-weeded and fertilized. It is also not unusual for an Amish woman to can as many as a thousand jars of fruits and vegetables in the late summer. The Amish person will gladly tell you that the Ordnung rules have little to do with food!

A typical Amish breakfast might include eggs, cornmeal mush, cooked cereal, and even fried potatoes. Bread, butter, and jelly are a staple at any meal. The dinner and supper menu will include meat, potatoes, and pastries–often rich in calories and fats. Dumplings, bean soup, and pickled beets will also be found on many Amish tables. For dessert there will always be a cake, pudding, pie, apple strudel, molasses doughnuts, or Dutch pancakes. The rich and sweet shoo-fly pie is a favorite in any Amish home. Some Amish women have been said to bake up to forty-five pies a day. They also brew their own root beer, ginger ale, and make their own popcorn and potato chips. Dinner can include schnitzel, kraut, or even Husband's Delight (beef, cheese and noodle casserole.)

> **SHOO-FLY PIE**
>
> The Pennsylvania Amish love this sweet candy-like coffee-cake with its gooey molasses texture.
>
> Mix for crumbs: (reserve ½ for top)
> 2/3 cup brown sugar
> 1 T. shortening
> 1 c. flour
>
> Filling:
> 1 c. molasses
> 3/4 c. boiling water
> 1 beaten egg
> 1 T. baking soda
>
> Combine soda with boiling water. Add egg and syrup. Add crumb mixture. Place into unbaked pie crust and cover with reserved crumbs. Bake at 375° for 10 minutes, then reduce heat to 350° and bake for an additional 35-45 minutes until firm.

Meals always begin and end with a table prayer. Family members sit quietly with heads bowed for a long period of time as each individual prays his or her own silent table prayer, often followed with the Lord's Prayer. The seating arrangement at the Amish table also holds significance. Traditionally the father sits at one end next to his wife. Boys often line the table next to the father, from youngest to oldest. Girls go around the other side also from youngest to oldest. Conversation is often about the chores that need to be completed or some other important part of the busy daily schedule.

Barn Raisings

Caring and sharing are an integral part of Amish life. Although remaining distant from the world, the Amish have always been willing to come to the rescue of anyone who is in need of their help, Amish or not. The Amish are quick to respond to their fellow brothers and sisters when help is needed, for weddings, funerals, or with the milking or harvesting chores of an ill neighbor. Those responses are woven into the Amish character and are an integral part of their life of obligation and duty toward one another.

This can clearly be seen in their barn raisings. One of the greatest disasters that can strike an Amish family is the loss of a barn. Fires and storms have destroyed many Amish barns, yet the community is always ready at a moment's notice to chip in and get that family back to work as quickly as possible. On barn raising day the entire community comes to help. Children assist the men, who use their expert skills in craftsmanship and building. The entire barn is built with hand tools. The barn consists of solid timber with mortise and tendon joints, making a frame that is very sound. As much as 25,000 board feet of lumber, 150 pounds of spikes and another 100 pounds of siding nails can go into the construction of one barn.[9] Women also come to prepare food for the hardworking men and often spend the afternoon quilting a masterpiece for the couple whose barn is being built. It is not unusual to have an entire barn built from foundation to shingles in a single day.

Language

The language of the Amish is a very real sign that these people are intent on maintaining their cultural heritage as well as separating themselves from the world. Through their use of a distinct language they build a wall between themselves and the rest of society. The Amish speak three languages, with elements of each flowing into the other two. As Amish children grow older, they move from one language to the next. Their basic spoken language is called Pennsylvania Dutch or Pennsylvania German. This is really a misnomer because it is not the same as that spoken by the Dutch people. Rather it resembles the German dialect spoken in the Palatine area of Germany. It would be more correct to call it the Pennsylvania Deutsch (Deitsch) or German language. In daily conversation around the kitchen table, at recess in the schoolyard, around the quilting circle, or among men discussing some issue, one will hear this common dialect. However, it is essentially a spoken language, and the Amish do not use it for their written correspondence.[10]

When children are old enough to attend school, they begin to learn English as their second language. This will be necessary for them to function in the business and occupational world. When they shop, speak on the telephone, or bargain over prices, they must be able to communicate. Many Amish are very concerned about their children using too much English and losing the German tradition. Some conversations among young people are a mixture of German and English, creating a dialect of its own. English is the primary language used by Amish for writing. Their newspapers and magazines are all printed in English.

> **HEX SIGNS**
> Many mistakenly think that the Amish paint the colorful geometric Hex Signs on their barns. But this is not true. These circular signs depicting birds, hearts and flowers were never a part of the Amish life, but rather originated in Pennsylvania by non-Amish religious groups known as the "fancy Dutch" people.

Because Amish children are taught English by individuals who have no more than an eighth grade education themselves, there is often a problem teaching its proper use. One Amish teacher mentioned the great difficulty she had in knowing how to pronounce certain English words. "Many English words are not pronounced the way they look," she wrote. "There is also a problem of knowing where to put the accent. Part of the reason for this is because much of our contact with the outside world is by reading rather than radio and television, so we don't hear words pronounced correctly...many times I have been embarrassed upon finding that for many years I have been saying a word wrong and didn't even know it...I have thought that it might be helpful for many of us if someone drew up a list of the most frequently mispronounced words among us Amish, and showed with accents and spelling what the correct pronunciation is."[11]

The third language of the Amish is used only in their worship services. Here a more pure form of High German is used. Their Bible readings (Luther's German Translation, which they use, was written in High German), prayers, sermons, and hymns are all spoken and sung in High German. Although Amish do not use High German for speaking, and many are not familiar with it apart from church, the young men chosen as pastors must learn to preach in High German.

Amish Names

Because Amish society is so close-knit, it is no surprise that the study of last names is very interesting. It is estimated that among the entire Amish population of nearly 200,000, there are less than 200 family names. Thus in one community there will likely be several people with the same first and last names. A study made in Lancaster County, Pennsylvania, found 115 Samuel Stoltzfuses, 115 Mary Stoltzfuses, 56 Mary Kings, and 52 John Kings. One rural mail carrier had three Amos E. Stoltzfuses and three Elam S. Stoltzfuses on the same route.[12]

Last names differ slightly from state to state. A study of frequently used names was made by John Hostetler in his book *Amish Society*. He discovered in Pennsylvania, for instance, the

Driving the Back Roads

five most frequently given last names were Stoltzfus (about 25%), King, Fischer, Beiler, and Lapp. In Ohio they were Miller (about 25%), Yoder, Troyer, Royer, and Herschberger. In Indiana they were Miller (about 25%), Yoder, Bontrager, Hochstetler, and Mast. Some of the most popular first names for boys were John, Eli, Levi, Amos, Samuel, and Joseph. For girls they were Mary, Rebecca, Katie, Anna, and Sarah.[13]

One solution to the confusion of names has been the use of nicknames. Many of them are very creative, however the nicknames are never used when speaking face to face. Some nicknames relate to the individual's husband or wife such as "Lomey Abe", nicknamed from his wife Salome. Sometimes they are merely shortened first names such as "Mose" for Moses or "Yonnie" for Jonathan. Many names are humorous or even derogatory such as "Limpy John", "Chubby Jonas", "Red Elmer", "Pepper Yonnie", "Chicken Elam", "Sewer Sam", or "Piggy Amos."[14] Although their names may not be flattering, they do depict the subtleness of Amish humor.

The Horse and Buggy

Perhaps the picture that best symbolizes the Amish lifestyle is the horse and buggy. This one item has done more to bring visitors to Amish country than anything else. The horse and buggy stand for the slow, deliberate character of the Amish, guided by Gelassenheit. The use of the horse and buggy places all sorts of limits on the people, and tells the world that as long as they drive their horses and buggies they are still quite separate from the world around them. Amish horse travel is usually limited to a distance of twenty-five miles a day. Likewise the use of horses for field work slows the pace of farm work to meet the horses' schedules. Using the work horse means no evening plowing and a maximum farm size of less than fifty acres. Horses also symbolize a more intimate connection with nature, which is held very dear to the Amish people. Whereas the use of automobiles brings with it a possible harmful influence because of speed, style, comfort, convenience, pride, expense of upkeep, insurance, and rising gas prices, the horse and buggy brings about a feeling of hominess, a close-knit family society, and harmony with God and nature.[15]

The horse and buggy we see in every Amish driveway and as a logo used by many Amish businesses did not always look like it does today. The present day buggy evolved over many years. From their beginning in the 1500's to the early 1800's, most Anabaptists traveled by foot or on horseback. Some used crude wagons or carts, but the carriages and buggies were left to the aristocrats. It wasn't until roads began to improve that the Amish started using horse-drawn vehicles. The Amish, never quick to accept any change, waited until the buggy was a commonplace item, and not considered as something reserved for the wealthy.

The earliest buggies were quite crude. Eventually springs were added and then tops. Each new change brought about a ripple effect within the church Ordnungs. Both the design of the buggy and their use of horses are closely regulated in their set of rules. Even seats with springs and use of dashboards caused problems within the communities.

A BUGGY RIDE
Who'd want to drive a motor car
When he could have a horse?
There may be many others, who
Would take a car, of course.

They do not know the joy of it,
A horse and buggy ride.
To feel the wind upon your face,
No stuffy seat inside.

Along the road we hear birds sing,
And watch a squirrel dash,
And just enjoy the scenery
Instead of rushing past.

The sound of horses' trotting feet
Is music to the ear.
No car is ever half as nice
At any time of year.

True, winter's snows are very cold
And rain makes me quite wet.
The wind can be uncomfortable-
Our fingers freeze, and yet

I still would choose a buggy ride,
In spite of cold or heat.
I shall insist that it is true,
A buggy can't be beat.
  16 year old author[16]

The buggies of today are built completely different from those of a hundred years ago. Standard buggies used today on the roads of Pennsylvania, Ohio, and Indiana include molded fiber glass boxes, sliding doors, roller bearing axles, hard rubber tires, battery operated headlamps, tail lights, clocks, speedometers, brakes, thermo-pane windows, windshield wipers, and comfortable carpeting throughout, not to mention some buggies with crushed velvet upholstery.

Most buggies are made by Amish craftsmen. Some "factories" may be as small as a one-man shop or they may employ a large workforce and can produce as many as 800 buggies a year. Often different shops produce the various parts of the buggies, such as the spoked wheels, shafts and running gear. Many hours go into the construction of a buggy, thus a price tag of $5000 is not unusual. Other than needing tire repair and spoke replacement, a good buggy will last many years. Most Amish men purchase three buggies in a lifetime. The first as a teenager, the second when their families grow in size to require a "two-seater", and the third when their family is older and they can once again get by with a traditional "one-seater" buggy.

By age nine Amish children begin to take the buggy out on the back roads, so that by age twelve they are skillful drivers. By age sixteen a boy gets his own buggy. A typical farm may have several buggies parked in the shed—one for each of the older sons and at least one for the family. Usually girls do not own their own buggies.[17] A seasoned young man can hitch up a horse and buggy in five minutes.

Standard buggy styles differ greatly from state to state and community to community. The design and color of the buggy is often dictated by church rules. All buggies within a community are the exact same because changes and personal variations are usually not allowed. Again the reason is to have everyone within the district appear the same–never rich or poor, never fancy or extravagant.

Basically there are three main buggy styles known as the Pennsylvania, Ohio, and Indiana. The Pennsylvania style buggy has straight sides and comes in yellow, black or gray. The most common color is the Lancaster gray top. The Nebraska Amish of Pennsylvania, a very conservative group, prefer either brown or white tops. Only kerosene lanterns are used to light the Nebraska buggies. Pennsylvania's Byler Amish drive yellow topped buggies, while the Renno Amish allow only black tops.

The Ohio Amish ride in buggies with angled sides and black tops. Many have roll curtains on the side windows, which help to keep out the cold and rain. Several Midwestern states such as Missouri, Wisconsin and Iowa use the Ohio style buggy.

The Amish in northern Indiana began using open buggies and eventually added the closed style. Indiana buggies also have angled sides. The black Indiana buggy top extends to just behind the seat, leaving the back of the buggy exposed while the Ohio buggy top extends all the way to the back of the buggy.[18]

Buggies or carriages aren't the only vehicles used by the Amish. Someone has estimated that there are at least ninety varieties of horse-drawn vehicles used throughout the United States by the Amish and Old Order Mennonites. Many Amish also own an open hack or spring wagon (so named because it has heavy duty springs for hauling heavy cargo.) The market wagon is an enclosed wagon–something like our station wagon–with a tailgate that swings up and a removable back seat. Courting was usually done in the open topped "courting buggy," however it seems that many young couples today prefer the closed top carriage. Beside these vehicles, the Amish communities also jointly own a cart used to carry their Sunday worship materials and a hearse for funerals.

The buggy horses used by the Amish are beautiful. Many of these horses were originally trained for harness racing and are from fine stock of bay colored Standard Bred horses sometimes costing as much as $2200 each. Many of these horses can be useful for up to twenty years.[19]

Local safety laws have been written especially for the Amish buggies and carriages. Today most communities demand that buggies be equipped with reflective tape, electric turn signals, flashers, fluorescent triangles, and electric headlamps. Some states also require license plates. There have been numerous accidents involving Amish buggies and automobiles, sometimes ending in injury or death. Many roads heavily traveled by the Amish now include special horse and buggy lanes. Most communities also post signs along the back roads that alert automobile drivers they are in buggy country.

Driving the Back Roads

1. Brad Igou, *The Amish in Their Own Words*, p. 233.
2. Donald B. Kraybill, *The Riddle of Amish Culture*, p. 60
3. John A. Hostetler, *Amish Society*, p. 240
4. Donald B. Kraybill, *The Riddle of Amish Culture*, p. 63.
5. Ibid. p. 67.
6. John A. Hostetler, *Amish Society*, p. 238
7. Donald B. Kraybill, *The Riddle of Amish Culture*, p. 68
8. Brad Igou, *The Amish in Their Own Words*, p. 362.
9. www.amishheartland.com.
10. John A. Hostetler, Amish Society, p. 242.
11. Sara E. Fischer and Rachel K. Stahl, *The Amish School*, p. 63.
12. Donald B. Kraybill, *The Riddle of Amish Culture*, p. 93.
13. John A. Hostetler, *Amish Society*, p. 245.
14. www.amishnews.com/amisharticles/nicknames.htm.
15. Stephen Scott, *Plain Buggies*, p. 6.
16. Joe Wittmer, *The Gentle People*, p. 29.
17. Stephen Scott, *Plain Buggies*, p. 12.
18. Ibid. p. 45.
19. Ibid. p. 26.

CHAPTER 9
An Amish Day

The Amish back roads are filled with activity. Children are hard at work mowing the lawn, doing the milking chores, or playing ball toss. Women are canning preserves, weeding the garden, and gathering eggs. Fathers and young men are repairing old and worn out machinery, hitching up the workhorses, or picking up stones that were plowed up in the fields. The Amish life is filled with chores from sun up to sundown, and sometimes even under the kerosene lamp after the sun sets. What do the Amish do that keeps their lives so busy? Are they any different from anyone else? What do they do for fun, and does this lifestyle give them an additional dose of good health? Let's travel down the back roads and take a close look into an Amish household.

A Day of Honest Housework

The Amish partnership of husband and wife runs along very scriptural and traditional gender lines. Each realizes his or her place in the order of God's plan, with the husband being the spiritual head of the house and the wife being submissive to the husband's authority. Each is loyal first to God and then to the mate. If either the husband or wife should be banned from the church community,

> "What can be lovelier and more beautiful than a home where husband and wife and children work together for the spiritual welfare of each other." One Amish woman's comment[1]

the mate will also shun the wayward husband or wife.

Amish couples do not stress the romantic side of their marriages as much as the outsiders do. Signs of affection are rarely seen in public. Instead, theirs is a loving, working relationship that seems to be strengthened by being with each other twenty-four hours a day.

As the spiritual head of the house, the husband is responsible for the religious training and welfare of his children. Although the wife is allowed to vote at church meetings and to help select ministers in the church, the man still holds all committee and ministerial positions. The female school teacher is perhaps the one exception to this rule, although today Amish men also serve as school teachers. The husband is also responsible for operating the farm and overseeing the work of the children in the barns and fields. He will, however, often help his wife in her home chores such as mowing the lawn and gardening. Since divorce is completely forbidden, most Amish couples know they must make their venture together do well or everything will fail and come to an abrupt halt.

The women are entrusted with the care of the family. They are responsible for the rearing of the little children, cooking, laundry, canning, sewing, washing, cleaning, and garden work. As a rule, laundry will be done on Monday, ironing on Tuesday, baking on Friday, and cleaning on Saturday. This is a huge task considering many Amish families have six or seven youngsters running around, several perhaps in need of diaper changing. Most Amish women are also without electric conveniences in the kitchen such as dishwasher, mixer, blender, or microwave, plus they don't have other time-saving devices as do modern households, like washers and dryers to help with the daily laundry. In addition to these chores, Amish housewives must also help with milking, butchering, and harvesting, and will likely serve as nurse and barber when called upon.

Gardens are a vital part of the Amish home. Beans, corn, cabbage, tomatoes, and celery are all staples of the Amish diet. In addition the Amish grow many fruits such as grapes, apples, plums, and cherries. Yarrow, St. John's Wort, and other herbs are also grown for medicinal purposes. And no Amish farm would be complete without a well-kept framework of beautiful flowers edging the gardens and walkways. Frequently older daughters in the family will help their mothers care for the garden; however, today more and more teens are expected to travel to town to earn money for themselves and the family. This puts an added responsibility on the mother of the household. To help with the family income, one Amish woman invited church groups into her home where she hosted a typical Amish dinner. She would seat up to fifty visitors in her kitchen and dining room and serve them an Amish feast. All this was done while keeping her five youngsters occupied.

Farming and Lunch-pail Work

To the Amish, farming is the preferred occupation. The land has always been regarded as an integral part of God's creation. In Genesis God told his people to till the soil, and the Amish have always attempted to follow God's design. (Some Amish will tell you that carpentry is the second-most respected occupation because Jesus himself was a carpenter.) The Amish farmers are regarded as experts in the art of running a productive farm. They have perfected ways to produce more crops per acre with far less energy than their "English" neighbors. A typical farm has about forty to fifty acres. Crops include wheat, corn, alfalfa, oats, rye, and tobacco. In past decades the Amish did not produce many cash crops, however that is beginning to change as some farmers have seen the necessity to increase their income. The grain crops are used mostly for feeding their horses, cows, pigs, sheep, and chickens.

Children are very helpful on the farms. Families blessed with several boys have an opportunity to run a large operation efficiently and effectively. Banks are more than willing to loan money to Amish farmers for new purchases, because they know the Amish will repay their loans.

Dairy farming is still a very popular livelihood among the Amish. In the past, farms generally milked fifteen to twenty cows, but with modern methods of generator-operated milking machines they can now milk forty to sixty cows. Amish dairy farmers have been forced to succumb to the policies and rules that regulate the dairy industry. However there are still a handful of Amish farmers who follow strict religious guidelines such as no milk pick up on Sundays. The Amish may not have registered livestock and do not belong to any dairy associations. They feel the excessive record keeping and competition could jeopardize their separation from the world.

Horses play a vital role in the field work. With the exception of a few farms that use gasoline-operated hay balers, corn pickers, or silo elevators, the horse is necessary to operate an Amish farm. The Amish care for their horses as if they were members of the family. Most farms have about six Belgian draft horses.

Land is usually handed down to the sons. Often the youngest son receives the farm because he is the last one left to farm that land. Amish farmers refuse any government subsidies for their land.

Yet beneath the surface of this otherwise idyllic world, there are severe problems. Over the past fifty years there has been less and less farm land available. With the Amish population doubling approximately every twenty years, the price of land increasing, and the profitability decreasing, many Amish have found it necessary to seek employment away from the farm. Today it is estimated that nearly two-thirds of Amish men are now employed elsewhere or run a home business not connected with farming. In one northern Indiana settlement, an Amish farmer remarked that his was the last family still tilling the soil. (In his church district, nearly 70% of the Amish men worked for a major manufacturer of motor homes.) This remarkable change happened in little over one generation. To many Amish families the change was devastating. Many felt outside employment could result in the demise of the Amish culture. Since the male role model was taken from the home for most of the waking hours, the bond between the father and his family would be weakened. Families might become smaller because there would not be the need for the children to help with the farm chores. Also, because the man was now employed away from home, he would have to work overtime, keep unusual schedules that take him away from important community events, and receive fringe benefits such as insurance and retirement funds that would entice him away from dependency on the community.

The first answer to this problem was to subdivide the farms among the children. However that served only as a short term solution. Instead, many Amish men packed their lunch-pails and headed elsewhere for employment. Many Amish men went to work in factories, but this brought with it a unique set of problems including having to work beside women, being forced to listen to "factory language," and becoming involved with the worldly problems of running a big business.

Eventually many Amish entrepreneurs decided it would be far better to operate a home business that would give them an opportunity to stay close to their families, to continue to farm what little acreage they had, and hopefully to bring in additional income. As a result hundreds of "micro-enterprises" were started. Today, in the Lancaster County area alone, there are an estimated 2000 thriving Amish-owned businesses. There are horse harness and wheel repair shops, dry goods and grocery stores, and furniture making enterprises. There are also Amish specialists serving as carpenters, printers, bakers, blacksmiths, butchers, toy makers, tombstone engravers, quilters, and many other occupations. Outsiders who buy Amish goods appreciate the high quality of materials they produce. Reading through the lists of Amish owned businesses in local directories one might even find bookkeeping and financial management listings. The Amish will not be interested in professional occupations such as a doctor or lawyer because they require additional schooling. High tech occupations like automobile repair, computer technology, and electronics would also be avoided. The Amish resourcefulness of beginning these home businesses has resulted in some success. Many Amish operate successful businesses, all without the aid of a high school diploma, electricity, or professional courses in money management or marketing. The failure rate of these new businesses is less than 5% as compared to the national rate of 60%.[2]

Another group of Amish men and women are employed at larger Amish owned factories where they can work alongside their own people. Some of these industries have grown to be multi-million dollar businesses that manufacture farm equipment, furniture, or cabinetry. Low overhead, low wages, little advertising, hard work, and good quality are all ingredients for the success of these Amish enterprises.

Yet another group of Amish men are site workers. These work crews are hired to build sheds, barns, and other buildings for people outside the Amish community. Each morning and evening Amish workers are driven to and from the work site. Because of the competitiveness of this occupation, some Amish districts have agreed to let these work crews use modern tools, equipment, and vehicles, but only at the work site.

Amish are considered very frugal. Since they are self-sufficient, their purchases are few and well planned. Yet there are times when they need to borrow money to make major purchases for land or buildings. The Amish are not against borrowing or keeping money in a bank account. However, because they feel the Scriptures speak against earning interest on their savings, many Amish give that money to the needy or the church.

> **AMISH AID COMMITTEES**
> (This is a list of some committees established by the Amish)
>
> Amish Aid Society
>   (Fire and storm aid)
> Amish Book Committee
>   (Amish book committee)
> Old Order Book Society
>   (Coordination of schools)
> Amish Liability Aid
>   (Liability assistance)
> National Steering Committee
>   (Government liaison)
> Amish Church Aid
>   (Medical assistance)
> Disaster Aid
>   (Disaster assistance)
> Product Liability Aid
>   (Liability assistance)
> Helping Hand
>   (Financial loans)
> People's Helpers
>   (Mental illness counseling)
> Safety Committee
>   (Farm and shop safety)[3]

The Amish do pay state, local and federal taxes, however, because they believe the church, not the state, should care for those in need, the Amish have been exempted from paying Social Security tax. They argued that if they refuse to accept Social Security, why should they pay it? Insurance is viewed as a risk that destroys a person's dependence on the church.

The Amish have, however, established several very loosely formed networks to help fellow Amish. Each committee is free from a central bureaucracy yet they function well when called upon. They are financed in various ways, from assessments based on tax payments to regular donations.

The Amish carry out their money affairs in secrecy, basing their decision on Matthew 6, where Jesus says to give, but give secretly. Those who are wealthy should be careful not to flaunt their riches in their lifestyles. Here again they believe Scripture tells them to abstain from luxuries as mentioned in 1 John 2:16, 17, "For everything in the world–the cravings of the sinful man, the lust of his eyes and the boasting of what he has and does– comes not from the Father but from the world. The world and its desires pass away, but the man who does the will of God lives forever." However, one might get a different impression driving the back roads and viewing some of the beautiful new Amish homes being built.

Recreation and Relaxation

Many younger children today rely on toys that blink, flash, talk, and burp, while the older children rely on their television and computer games. If there aren't batteries or if it isn't plugged in, the toy is considered worthless. Amish children are different. They entertain themselves with card games, balls, clapping games, and other indoor play to pass their time. Outdoor fun includes swimming in the creek, playing ball, building tunnels, or riding bikes. Older children sometimes play *Mosch Balle* (mush ball or corner ball), a game much like dodge ball, where boys positioned at four corners throw a ball at a person in the middle. *Botching* is another popular game where two children seated opposite each other clap their hands and knees together rapidly.

In summer many Amish boys and girls are involved in community softball games. Some church districts even allow uniforms.

Adults pass their leisure time smoking cigars (cigarettes are prohibited in most districts), quilting, or reading one of their Amish periodicals like *The Budget* or *Die Botschaft.* These newspapers read like one long chain letter where Amish writers, called scribes, report from all over the country on personal news such as weddings, injuries, illness, and just common conversation about the weather, crops, and families. For anyone wanting to learn about Amish life, these papers provide a very clear picture. Many homes also have bookshelves filled with copies of *Reader's Digest* books or other fiction novels. Men enjoy attending auctions where they can catch up on the latest local news.

A favorite of Amish families is the "frolic." A frolic is a get-together where Amish throughout the community gather for a community project such as cleaning a new house or working at the schoolyard. The frolic gives everyone an opportunity to enjoy fellowship while working together on a worthwhile project. Amish women also follow the tradition of "Sister's Day," an opportunity for the ladies to get together as they tell family stories and share homemaking secrets and ideas.

It is not unusual for Amish to take extended vacation trips around the country to visit historical places, or national parks. Several families often vacation together. They will need the help of the "English" to provide the transportation

The Amish observe church holidays like other Christians, yet they always do it with restraint. Christmas is not nearly as special to the Amish as it is to others. Never would an Amish man cut down a beautiful pine tree just to decorate his parlor. Gifts also do not play a very important part of the Amish Christmas. At most, children might find a plate of cookies, homemade candy, or perhaps a store-bought candy bar or bag of potato chips awaiting them on Christmas morning. Often the father will read the Christmas story to the family before the morning chores. If gifts are exchanged they are usually handmade projects that mom and dad had been secretly making. A tradition that still continues in many Amish homes is celebrating "Old Christmas" on January 6th with feasting and family visits. The Amish also observe Good Friday, Easter, Ascension Day, Pentecost, and Thanksgiving. Good Friday and fall and spring communion are not nearly as much fun for the children, since the Amish fast during these days.

Holidays not observed by the Amish include Memorial Day, Veterans' Day, Labor Day, and the 4th of July. These national holidays do not agree with the Amish view of abstaining from government involvement. Although celebrating Halloween is also not permitted, pumpkins may be seen on some Amish porches.

The Amish celebrate holidays throughout the year and enjoy their own type of recreation and relaxation. Unlike the impression they often give as a stern and serious people, the Amish do not lack for fun and games. Yet, they are careful to keep restrictions on the extent of their fun, keeping well within the boundaries of their religion.

Health

There has long been a misunderstanding that the Plain People refuse outside medical assistance. The Amish do not oppose medicine or medical treatment. Nothing in the Bible forbids them from making use of outside medical services. However, when the Amish are in need of medical help, they must rely on outsiders since there are no Amish physicians, surgeons, psychologists, or dentists. A non-Amish doctor who lives within the Amish community and serves their needs is always welcome. This can bring the doctor unique challenges like trying to communicate with Amish children who do not yet speak English. Many Amish who leave the community often do so to study medicine.

The Amish believe that healing is a gift of God. Only he can bring about healing through the medication or treatment. Thus their lives are always in the hands of God, because it is God who gives life and God who takes it away.

SOME AILMENTS ADDRESSED BY VARIOUS ALL NATURAL PRODUCTS ADVERTISED IN THE AMISH NEWSPAPER "THE BUDGET"[4]
... a natural antibiotic
... relief for stress
... immune system strengthener
... a salve for any human or beast
... sinus problem control
... eliminates candida
... rids your body of dead worms
... lower high blood pressure
... cures Hepatitus B & C
... morning sickness balm
... anti-aging fruit and mineral drink
... levels sugar and glucose
... cranial treatment
... liver detoxin
... pinworm medicine
... cure for skin eruptions

Folk Medicine

Although the Amish make use of outside medical services they also advocate home remedies and natural cures. Amish newspapers are filled with ads from ointments to salves, from poultices to teas and tonics. Although many of these therapies do contain valid healing properties, many Amish have been deceived by false claims and advertising. It is not unusual for an Amish person to travel hundreds of miles to spend time in a healing spa or hot-spring, or to be treated with a cure not sanctioned in the United States. Chiropractic care and reflexology are also used frequently. A little-known health remedy of the Pennsylvania Dutch, including the Amish and Old Order Mennonites, was the use of a *Brauche* for their "powwowing" or "sympathy healing". A *Brauche* is an Amish individual who performs rituals and other "skills" such as spiritualistic incantations at the bed of the sick person. Although many Amish deny its use today, there is evidence that it is still being practiced secretly in some Amish circles, yet it is now often referred to as "faith healing."[5]

Hospital Treatment

The Amish, like everyone else, sometimes need hospital treatment. Records indicate they do not always practice worthwhile preventative measures in their diet or in their everyday work life. They also have a history of not seeking professional healthcare in time, which often has fatal results. Certainly the fact that many still work on farms and have many children involved in that sometimes dangerous work does attribute something to the need for constant medical care. A reliable local doctor is treasured in any Amish community. Since there is no health insurance for the Amish, medical bills must be paid by the families, the church districts, or even the church at large.

As previously mentioned, the Amish keep in touch through two newspapers, *The Budget* and *Die Botschaft*. Recent issues included these health related stories from the back roads of Amish country.

- A ten year old boy mistakenly drank clear peroxide. One day stay in hospital.
- A four year old girl was hospitalized for jumping from a wagon onto a fork, breaking her arm and getting an infection.
- A young man got kicked by a horse and broke both bones in his one leg.
- An elderly farmer had a bout with a cow and broke a chip off his knee.
- A young woman was bitten by a copperhead snake while disking the field. She couldn't walk for three days.
- A teenager was kicked in the face by a horse. He had a lot of stitches and lost some teeth so he spent the night in the emergency room.
- A young lad fell out of a tree and broke his left arm. A year ago he fell out of another tree and broke his right arm.
- A farmer was kicked in the chest by a horse "and was soon gone."
- A young man fell from a wagon load of hay onto the concrete and had both wrists crushed.
- A twelve year old fell and was dragged by a horse. He was taken to emergency via ambulance where he was "x-rayed, glued and sent home."
- A five year old fell down a silo chute and broke his leg below the knee.
- An elderly Amish woman broke either her arm or her collar bone last week when she got off a buggy.

- A two year old boy toppled out of a carriage. At first his parents thought they drove over him with the back wheel but afterward decided they did not.

Today immunization is carried out in Amish communities, however, lack of immunization in the past has caused some health problems. In 1979 there was a major outbreak of polio in several Amish communities where there were few immunized children. It was then that the Amish realized the importance of immunization against such diseases.

Hereditary Diseases

The Amish and the Hutterites are inbred people, and provide a perfect community in which to study the effects of hereditary diseases. The Amish of Lancaster County can be traced to just 200 Swiss Anabaptists who landed on the shores of Pennsylvania in the 1700's. Since the Amish forbid marriage outside the community, they have remained essentially closed to outsiders for the past twelve generations. As a result the Amish suffer from several genetic diseases that have little effect on the rest of the population. This is caused by what researchers call the "founder effect". It is thought that after several generations of intermarriage, rare genetic flaws begin to surface. Although most individuals carry many of these flaws, they do not become apparent in the offspring until one marries someone with the same rare genetic flaws.[6] This effect is becoming more and more apparent as researchers attempt to find cures for dozens of genetic diseases that have surfaced in the Amish community. Fortunately the Amish have been very willing to cooperate with testing and research for these disorders.

As one reads through the many articles in the Amish periodicals, it is startling to see comments regarding children who are afflicted with "an extra finger on each hand", "an enzyme that is missing", "a bleeder", or a "cleft lip". It is also not unusual to read the sad news of yet another stillborn child.

A major genetic disease is "maple syrup urine disease," which is so named because the patient's urine and earwax take on the smell of maple syrup. This treatable disease is connected with a protein disorder and can cause irreversible brain damage in infants as young as one week old.

Another genetic disease that affects children is "glutaric aciduria type 1" (too much acid in the blood and body tissue). These youngsters start out life seemingly healthy, but if they become sick with something as minor as a common cold, they could suffer permanent brain damage within hours.

Yet another problem affecting many Amish today is "Ellis-van Creveld syndrome." This rare disorder is the cause of short-limbed dwarfism. Although many stillborn babies have been diagnosed with this syndrome, those that survive may also have additional fingers and toes, cleft lip and malformation of wrist bones and fingernails. Dwarfism is fairly common in some Amish settlements.

Hemophelia, certain types of muscular dystrophy, and other rare diseases have also been found more frequently in Amish districts than elsewhere in the United States.

The Amish are aware of these problems, which are occurring with greater regularity. One Amish gentleman said, "The best gift we can bestow upon future generations is to make every intelligent effort within our power and ability to ensure that they do not inherit genetic weaknesses from us...Given enough time, this [inbreeding] is almost a sure formula to genetic disaster...Church leaders and parents need to recognize that it is important for a community to have genetic diversity."[7]

If discovered in the early stages, many of these diseases are treatable. Today many Amish communities are constructing clinics that are easily accessible for the horse and buggy people.

Mental Illness

Many outsiders think that because the Amish live such a carefree style of life, they should be relatively free of mental illness. That simply is not the case. Mental illness and suicide affect the Amish family just as they do the general population. Ironically, the religion of these people can have a tendency to bring about unusual stress and anxiety. The role of women in the home often frustrates them because they cannot express their feelings and are not free to discuss important matters with their husbands. Consequently, many Amish women suffer from depression. Many young men who are newly elected to a church or community position have a difficult time dealing with the pressures put on them by the community patriarchs. The pressures of living in a society of rules and regulations, unquestioned power of church leaders, parents who can be overly strict in the homes, and the ever-increasing challenge of avoiding the world around them can bring about stress that sometimes leads to a breaking point.

The Amish usually care for the mentally ill in the home, however, there are some Amish communities that have built special homes for those with extreme mental health problems. Families and the community are very supportive of anyone who suffers any form of illness. However, they also believe that whatever happens in this life is because of the will of God.

Funerals

As with birth and marriage, death meets the Amish in a very simple and natural way. There are no flower arrangements, no eulogies or carved monuments. Rather, death is viewed as the natural process that leads everyone from temporal to

> **WHY?**
> From a mother whose child died shortly after birth.
>
> "Of course, all the time the question 'Why?' comes to our minds. But we should not expect to be able to understand everything in this life, and should never put a question mark where God has put a period."[8]

eternal life. This is not to say that those who have died are not sorely missed, or that their lives were simply lived in vain. There is a great respect for life and death within the Amish community, and the community suffers together during any illness or death. The Amish community is very close. Those who are gravely ill receive special visits by friends and relatives. Visits may be short, but they all leave the message that there is love and care for the ailing. Most Amish die at home. Although the Amish do not reject medical attention at the local hospital, they much prefer to be at home when they take their final breath. Whenever there is a death it affects everyone within the church district and in the surrounding areas as well.

News of a death in the community spreads quickly. The funeral customarily takes place three days after death. An undertaker is called to care for the body in keeping with state law. They embalm the body, however, there is no use of any cosmetics. The deceased is returned to the home within a few hours. (Autopsies are never allowed.) All of the preparations for the burial are done with little expense to the family, for it is the community that takes upon itself these responsibilities. Six nephews are often given the honor and responsibility to serve as the pallbearers and grave diggers. Six non-related, unmarried, young men and women are also selected to be the "chore boys" and "chore girls". Their responsibility is to see that the home life of the departed one's family continues to run smoothly–that meals are cooked, and cows are fed and milked–while the family takes time for the funeral. They continue to assist for a number of days after the funeral.[8]

The six-sided wooden casket is often lined with white and has a hinged door on the upper torso for viewing the body. There are no side handles on Amish caskets. Ornate carving and fancy lining in the coffin is not permitted. The individual is presented in white clothes signifying purity in Christ's resurrection. (Women are often buried in their wedding cape, apron and hat.)

The casket is placed in the living room or a bedroom. Usually a kerosene lamp burns day and night next to the coffin. Some Amish communities still observe a twenty-four hour wake, in which a relative stays with the body at all hours of the day. A steady stream of visitors comes to pay their respects during the two days prior to the funeral.

At the funeral service the casket is closed. The nearly two-hour service includes spoken hymns (never sung), plus several sermons. Often ministers and bishops from neighboring communities also attend. There are never flowers at an Amish funeral and there are never any spoken eulogies, for it would not be right to give special honor to the deceased. After the service has ended, the mourners make their way to the cemetery in a long winding procession of black carriages. The procession is led by a black hearse carriage designed especially for that purpose. There is a brief viewing at the gravesite before the body is lowered into the hand-dug grave. The family then returns to the home for refreshment and fellowship. Often this fellowship meal will have several hundred guests. Funerals are seen as the ultimate surrender to God. It is purely Gelassenheit!

The grave will be marked by a small gravestone with only name and dates etched into it. Often the markers are made by loving family members. Monuments could never be considered for they would again bring unnecessary attention to the individual. In death as well as in life it would be unconscionable to raise oneself above others.

A widow will mourn the passing of her husband by wearing a black dress for as much as a year. For many months relatives and friends will drop in to befriend the survivors.

Tourism

As unlikely as it may seem, tourism does play a major part in the lives of many Amish people. Time has certainly brought about change to the lush green valleys of Pennsylvania. Once considered some of the most fertile land in the United States, this area is now one of the busiest tourist regions in the country. How ironic that this people whose very religion teaches a life of remaining apart from the world, is now pursued by tourists who can't snap enough photos. Today the two most heavily traveled Amish tourist spots are in the Lancaster, Pennsylvania, area near the towns of Intercourse and Bird-in-Hand, and the Shipshewana area in northern Indiana.

The Lancaster region accommodates an estimated five million tourists each year, taking in millions of tourist dollars. The irony continues as tourists flock around the Amish people, trying desperately to get a photograph of a person whose religion teaches that to pose for a picture is to make a graven image of oneself. Some tourists have become so boorish as to open school doors while classes are in session.

Visitors to Lancaster County are often treated to bus tours, model farm homes to visit, movies about Amish life, buggy rides, and all sorts of Amish attractions, many of which are far from the real thing. The Amish tourist industry tries to keep tourists at a distance. However, some Amish have circumvented that protection and set up roadside stands where they sell vegetables, crafts and other original Amish goods and products.

In some ways the tourist industry has helped the Amish people. Not only is it a way to earn money, but it gives the Amish community a strong voice in public affairs. Pennsylvania now regards tourism as one of its most important industries. An Amish threat to move elsewhere would be devastating and thus public officials are very sympathetic to the Amish.

In other ways tourism has also brought about negative results. For a people whose desire is to be free of the outside world, tourism has brought them more into the spotlight. Land prices in tourist areas have skyrocketed to unbelievable levels. Big businesses have far greater resources at their disposal to purchase huge chunks of prime land for their tourist traps than do the Amish farmers to expand their fields. This has brought Amish growth in some areas to a standstill.

Yet many Amish see this as a way to conduct outreach as they witness to others through their simple and humble way of life.

1. Joe Wittmer, *The Gentle People: Personal Reflections of Amish Life Expanded Edition*, p. 53.
2. Donald B. Kraybill, *The Riddle of Amish Culture*, p. 256.
3. Donald B. Kraybill, *The Riddle of the Amish Culture*, p. 101.
4. *The Budget*, June 8, 2005.
5. John A. Hostetler, *Amish Society*, p. 336.
6. http://cbsnews.com/stories/2005/06/08/6011/main700519.shtml
7. Joe Wittmer, *The Gentle People: Personal Reflections of Amish Life*. p. 136
8. Brad Igou, *The Amish in Their Own Words*, p. 286.
9. Joe Wittmer, *The Gentle People: Personal Reflections of Amish Life,* p. 177.

CHAPTER 10
Personal Reflections

We have traveled the back roads in hopes of piecing together the puzzle of the Plain People. We've visited a culture quite unlike our own, a society whose very existence depends entirely on its separation from worldly influence. It is that conviction that keeps this culture from becoming just another ingredient in America's melting pot. Like other Christians, the Plain People strive to be in the world but not of it. Like other Christians, they realize the effects that this world can have on their faith. Yet unlike most other Christians, they feel that to live "in the world but not of it" means to completely avoid anyone or anything that was not shaped in the same mold as they. To accomplish this goal they established a society built on a foundation of rules. Not God's rules, but ones that rose from the traditions of their ancestors.

As we drove the back roads you may have felt an urge to copy the ways of the Plain People. It's not unusual for outsiders to envy their lifestyle and their strict and steady view of life. Certainly there is plenty to envy. Many of us long for a time and place where we can live our lives separate from the sins, lures, and entrapments of modern society. We can't help but agree with the hymn writer who said that "The world is very evil; the times are waxing late..." We often wish our families could simply withdraw to some secluded place to live out our lives with those of our faith and convictions. It almost seems that the

Amish have found that secret Utopia that we all have been searching for. But before we get overly zealous and sell everything to buy forty acres outside Goshen, Indiana, we might want to weigh the options. All is not quite as it appears on the surface. There are two sides to the Amish coin, and we would do well to look at both.

Up to now I have tried to stay as factual and neutral as possible. My hope was to give you a complete picture of Anabaptist society, especially the Amish way of life. I wanted you to taste the shoo-fly pie, attend an Amish wedding, take a ride in an Amish buggy, help with a barn raising, and sneak into an Amish school. It was an interesting journey. This chapter however will be different. It's time to pull back the covering and take a serious look behind the scenes.

It Seems So Good

The Anabaptists follow a line of people whose roots lie in the Reformation. The Lutheran church was born on October 31, 1517. Many others followed Luther's lead, and although they did not pattern their faith after his in every respect, they shared in the freedom and light of the gospel that began on that day in 1517. Their early leaders and members were among those who had long waited for a time when the Roman Catholic Church would be held accountable for their arrogance and careless handling of God's Word.

Less than a decade after Luther nailed the Ninety-five Theses on the church door in Wittenberg, the Anabaptists were organized. Although their movement lacked the leadership that was evident in the Lutheran and Swiss Reformation, they nevertheless were led to write down their teachings in the two major statements of faith, the Dordrecht Confession of Faith and the Schleitheim Articles. These two documents established their basic system of belief, and although serious theological problems would arise from their view of the government and the sacraments, they stood firmly on the depravity of the sinner, the need of a Savior, the forgiveness found in the blood of Jesus Christ, and the salvation in heaven belonging to those who believe and confess Jesus as Lord and Savior. The Anabaptists were willing to die for these truths. Even those who would not agree with all their theology would do well to emulate their commitment. Whether these convictions are still held 400 years later may be a valid question.

There are many areas of Amish life that we might do well to consider. The family is certainly one aspect that the Amish hold in high regard. In modern society, divorce, unwed mothers, children ruling the home, and fathers not accepting responsibility for their families, are far too common even among Christians. The Amish hold the family in high regard. Pre-marital sex is always a sin, divorce is forbidden, and marriage is only blessed if it is between two adults who share the same faith. These views are rigid and unmovable, and they reflect a deep and demanding respect for the family institution.

Likewise, the respect and care for the elderly is a positive part of the Amish life. Grandparents are cared for in the home where they can receive the help, love, and respect they have earned through years of trials and hard work. Their home is never farther away than through a doorway, and their words still carry the greatest weight because they speak from an experience that no one else can claim.

The role of the father is also important to the Amish. If there is one thing that concerns the Amish today, it is the fact that many fathers are no longer able to spend every waking hour at home with their families. To the Amish, the home is where dad belongs, and it's also where he wants to be! Theirs is a patriarchal society where there is an unquestioned respect for the father. He has the final say on important decisions, and he takes his role as head of the household seriously. In addition, the

Driving the Back Roads

Amish man's work ethic, expertise, and desire to do his best is clearly noticed by those around him.

Yet the Amish also know that the woman of the house is far more important than just for having babies. She is the glue that holds the family together. She sees to it that schedules are kept, meals are prepared, gardens are planted, clothes are mended, the sick are nursed, the home is cleaned and tidy, and in her "spare time" she still helps with barn chores and bookkeeping.

Amish children are also an integral part of Amish life. They are trained from early on to manage the many chores that must be done in order for the family to function. Milking the cows, gathering eggs, and cooking breakfast before school time, are accepted (although not always enjoyed) tasks. Unlike many "English" homes today, the Amish family is designed to run like a well-tuned engine, seldom skipping a beat. Fieldwork is hard for Amish boys, and learning to manage a family of their own is hard work for the girls as well. Yet the lives of Amish children are still filled with fun and games. They have the same sense of humor, love for practical joking, and need to tease their siblings that comes packaged in every child.

The Amish philosophy of humility or selflessness is another trait that deserves our attention. The Amish have turned topsy-turvy the world's whining of "me first" with their conviction that our purpose in this life is not to stand out above the rest, not to climb to the top of the social ladder, not to estimate when we will earn our first million, and not to be worshiped and praised, but rather to be of humble heart, quietly thanking the Maker who designed us. Too often we place our children (from very young on) on pedestals trying to prove that our kids are smarter, more athletic, better looking, more talented, and certainly more deserving of ribbons, awards and accolades, than all the rest. The Amish have rejected all that.

In a world of excess, Amish birthdays are celebrated, but with restraint. Gifts are given at Christmas time, but within reason. Weddings are joyous occasions, but without great expense and extravagance. Even in death the Amish show modesty by using headstones that are little more than plot markers. The Amish view of self and others is one of the most difficult elements for outsiders to deal with. Many who have tried to join the Amish religion have found that although it is possible to adjust to the Amish lifestyle and work ethic, the surrendering of oneself is nearly impossible to achieve. That is one area that needs to be inbred from little on.

All Is Not As It Seems

Without a doubt there are those Amish families who do not fit well into the Amish pattern. The Amish are not immune from dysfunctional homes, a fact that is readily picked up by the local media that loves to get its hands on the Amish father who mistreated his children, the young Amish boy who was arrested for drug abuse, and the Amish girl who got pregnant. Sadly these things do happen in Amish society. They are not exempt from any of the sins that lie hidden in everyone's heart. It would be a travesty not to admit these failures and many others that are a part of Amish culture. The Amish are no more immune from the wiles of Satan than anyone else. Living in seclusion does not mean that Satan simply leaves them alone.

Problems with the Government

The Anabaptist view of the establishment and purpose of earthly government, oath taking, suing in a court of law, running for office, voting, or serving in the military, has been the cause of much of their pain and persecution. Their pacifist reasoning is based on the view that as Christians we now have become heavenly citizens of a spiritual kingdom; that we now fight with spiritual weapons; that Christ never wished to be an earthly King; that Christ always withheld force, and always turned the other cheek.

What is sadly missed with this line of thinking is that when we became Christians we became members of two societies. We believe with the Anabaptist that in Christ we are honored and privileged to hold citizenship in his heavenly kingdom. That reality is here with us now and will be manifest more when we enter the gates of heaven.

However, we are citizens of earthly kingdoms which are also established by God. The powers that be in earthly kingdoms are there to maintain peace and serve justice on those who do wrong. Nowhere does Scripture tell us to avoid any involvement with the government. God gives us the right and the responsibility to serve as police officers, fight in the military, run for public office, and vote in elections. The Bible contains many instances of God's people serving in government positions and bearing arms. David was not a conscientious objector, and Daniel did not refuse serving the king of Babylon. The Syrian commander Naaman, and the jailer at Philippi were never told to quit their military service in order to serve God. The Amish enjoy the blessing of a peaceful nation, often won with the blood of soldiers who fight on the field of battle. The fact that they refuse to serve in the military has been a source of contention between them and the secular powers God has ordained.

Too Difficult to Discuss

No matter which area of Anabaptist beliefs you study, you will always come back to their doctrines of Holy Baptism and the Lord's Supper. The subject of the sacraments is difficult to discuss with an Anabaptist, because they have none. Anabaptists consider sacraments not as a means by which God imparts his grace, but rather as "rituals", "symbols" or "signs" of God's grace. To the Anabaptist, the Lord's Supper is a rite celebrated a few times each year that serves as a remembrance of the shedding of Christ's blood. In a conversation with a Mennonite pastor I was asked how many times my church celebrates the

Lord's Supper. I told him every other week. He appreciated the idea, because, he said, it is good for the people to be drawn back more often to the crucifixion. But, I explained, that wasn't the only reason Christians should celebrate the Lord's Supper. Instead it has much more to do with our sins and the actual body and blood that Christ now shares with his believing family.

Baptism is also difficult to discuss with Anabaptists. Like Ulrich Zwingli and the Swiss Reformers, the Anabaptists believe that baptism is not a means through which God gives his grace, but an outward sign. It has become a rite of passage from being a secondary citizen of the church (as they were when they were children), to being a bona fide member who promises sacrificial allegiance to the Amish cause. It has little to do with what God does for them, and very much to do with what they must do for God.

In lieu of baptism, the Amish feel in some magical way God gives their children an invisible shield that protects them from the curse of their sins. How ironic that a church body that expends so great an effort to keep their children away from the influences of the sinful world, shows such great reluctance to give their children the blessing of baptism. Their claim that the Bible nowhere mentions infant baptism is simply not true. Jesus himself commanded us to "Go and make disciples *of all nations*, baptizing them..." (Matthew 28:19), and again, "...she *and the members of her household* were baptized..." (Acts 16:15), and "He *and all his family* were baptized" (Acts 16:33). Children are indeed a part of Christ's command. We also know that children are sinful, and in need of forgiveness: "I tell you the truth, *no one* can enter the kingdom of God unless he is born of water and the Spirit. Flesh gives birth to flesh, but Spirit gives birth to spirit" (John 3:4, 5), and "surely *I was sinful at birth,* sinful from the time my mother conceived me" (Psalm 51:5). Children also have the ability to believe in their loving Lord. "But if anyone causes one of *these little ones who believe in me* to sin..."

(Matthew 18:6) Thus the arguments that children cannot believe, are not able to sin, are protected until they come of age, or are not specifically mentioned in God's Word are simply not true.

Never Certain of Salvation

Although most Amish remain faithful to their baptismal promise, there are many Amish who have chosen to leave the strict lifestyle behind. "Jumping the fence" or "crossing over" are terms often used for those who have left the Amish settlement to live with the "worldly". When asked to give a reason for jumping the fence, they say things like, "Christianity is supposed to be about the love of Christ, not the laws of a church," and, "there is too much emphasis on appearance–not on personal faith."

One of the most disconcerting areas of the Amish life is an almost complete focus on the rules, and the absence of any real assurance of salvation. Ruth Irene Garrett writes in her book, *Crossing Over,* "The Amish believe that by works and deeds they might find themselves worthy in God's good graces to go to heaven. Ask any Amish if they're going to heaven, and they'll say, 'That's not my choice. That's God's choice.' They can never be sure they're going, because they might misstep between now and the moment they die."[1]

Amish writings repeatedly mention that although they appear cold and serious on the outside, inwardly they are really a happy people. To some extent this may be true. Although they live hard lives, they do seem content with their lot in life. Yet if we define true happiness as the joy found in the assurance of salvation, then I maintain that the Amish are missing something very important. Throughout their lives, the Amish are taught to believe that it is a sin to assume they will receive their eternal reward in heaven. To do so would be presumptuous, asserting their will over God's will. Consequently they live their lives in the anticipation that if they continue to sacrifice themselves to the Lord, he will rule in their favor on judgment day. Theirs is a life void of true Christian joy found in the confidence, hope, and assurance of salvation.

Beverly Lewis, a well-known author who has topped Christian fiction charts with her *Lancaster County* books, spent years studying and speaking with the Amish people of Lancaster County, Pennsylvania. In my correspondence with her, she made some rather startling comments:

> "The Amish themselves will tell you quite plainly that they do not embrace the assurance of salvation, simply the hope of salvation. They believe that they cannot know if they are saved in this life, but only on the judgment day; and for a person to claim salvation would be heretical, and put him on dangerous ground of losing his eternal soul. Why? Because such talk smacks with pride, one of their greatest fears. The question is often asked: how can Amish continue to reject modern conveniences, etc., in short, live, dress, and conduct their lives the way they do, if they do not know the Lord Jesus as their personal Savior and Lord? In other words, wouldn't it require knowing Christ in an intimate way, embracing his shed blood as the only covering for sin, walking with him on a daily basis, to be able to endure such a culture? The answer undoubtedly, is steeped in 300 years of tradition–doing things the same way, adhering to the bishop's rulings, and, in many cases–if those expectations are ignored–then being excommunicated and shunned from family, friends, and the church community." (Used by permission of Beverly Lewis.)

It is a fact that many Amish lives have become so clouded with their tradition, rules, Ordnung, and Gelassenheit, that they have lost sight of the glorious light of the Gospel. Instead of walking in the assurance and the hope of salvation that the

Gospel message provides, their path is filled with sacrifice, doing right, and adhering to the rules of the church for fear that if they don't, either the church will cease to exist or they will be forever shunned. Their energy is spent on keeping the community together at any cost, even if it means losing their grasp on "the one thing needful" and the promise it provides.

God Is a Gracious God

In my entire library of Amish literature, there are two areas that are rarely mentioned: grace and love. These two necessary elements of God's plan of salvation are sadly missing in their lives. First there is a fear in even approaching a discussion of God's grace. "Yes, we believe in grace, BUT..." is their standard comment. They simply cannot resign themselves to the fact that God's grace is all that is necessary for salvation. God did not write any "buts" into his plan. "My grace is sufficient" is the way God put it. Yet to the Amish that grace must always be accompanied by works. They simply cannot allow God to do the saving. They always feel it is necessary that they do something to earn that salvation. In a letter written to me by a Mennonite pastor regarding this subject, he wrote, "Grace isn't always understood [among the Amish] as well as it might be. There may be an underlying fear that persons would stray too far from the conventional rules if grace is too abundant. The Amish vary on these understandings from the very strict to the more lenient grace observing ones."

Plain People feel they must add works to God's grace to make it complete. Where Luther claimed that works are a result or complement to the grace of God, the Plain People make them a requirement or necessity to earn God's grace. In their quest to live lives of humility, brow beating, sacrificing, and rule following, some have begun to look like the Pharisees in Christ's day. Their lives have become so wrapped up in rules that they now look to the rest of the world and say, "Look what we've become. See the sacrificial lives we live." This is clearly shown in the rules they have placed upon themselves. Limited education, dress, housing, farming, child rearing, are all man-made rules not found in Scripture. Their people are not even allowed to study the Bible for fear that that would be questioning God's authority. Some Amish say that if someone begins reading the Bible regularly, it means they are preparing to leave.

Intimidation and Fear

The Amish system of practices and beliefs is driven by fear and carried out by intimidation. Living under the dark threat of not only being excommunicated from the church but being shunned by family, friends, and community, the Plain People faithfully listen to sermons based on Law, abide by the Ordnung of their church, and try their best not to question anything. Even their refusal to do mission work reflects on the fear that they may encounter people from other religions who might tear them away from their church community.

The overriding fear is that the church district will crumble. This fear manifests itself in a list of controlling rules that assure that no one will be able to stray too far from the safety of the church. Fences are built around their dress, their education, their travel, their lifestyles, their language, their family life, their worship, their desire to evangelize, all because of fear.

Some of their fear comes from a lack of confidence in truly understanding God's Word. They are not confident that they even know the basics of God's Word. Some of this is caused by their limited education. Consider that this society is only made up of people who have a grade school education, and although there is nothing wrong with their limited schooling, remember that these people are forbidden to advance beyond that point. Their teachers have only an eighth grade education. Their ministers, deacons, and bishops also have only an eighth grade education. This results in a very limited amount of basic knowledge not only of the world around them, but of God's Word as well. Most societies that limit education do so to keep their people from becoming too knowledgeable about those around them. They realize the danger of their people knowing too much. One way the Amish keep their people from becoming too aware of the world is to intimidate them with wild stories of what might lie "out there in the world". In some cases outlandish accounts have been passed on by Amish who indoctrinate their children into believing that the sinful world is destined to destroy them and if they venture beyond the confines of their community they will immediately be overtaken.

The ultimate portrayal of this fear is the *Meidung* or ban. As long as one stays within the guidelines of the church one might attain salvation, but leaving that community means to be immediately cut off from God. Every Amish is taught that once excommunicated, the soul is destined for hell and damnation. Perhaps this is a major reason behind the high percentage of children that remain within the Amish community, and also why so few baptized Amish ever leave.

God Is a Loving God

Love is another concept quite foreign to the Amish. It is startling to realize that in their Pennsylvania Dutch language there is no word for "love".[2] The word is rarely spoken in Amish homes and even more rarely shown. Hugs and kisses are all too rare between husbands and wives or parents and children. At best one might hear a faint whisper of God's love now and again.

Reading the Amish newspapers and other periodicals is an interesting experience. They give a marvelous glimpse into the hearts and souls of these people. The hundreds of personal letters reflect their way of life in a candid and open setting. But the more one reads, the more one discovers that of the many Bible passages quoted, nearly all of them deal with what we should and should not do. They all repeat the same theme that God's laws need to be followed. There is little evidence of God's love and faithfulness. While trying so hard to follow Christ's command to take up their crosses and follow him, they have forgotten who it is they are following. John wrote, "This is how we know what love is: Jesus Christ laid down his life for us," (1 John 3:16). Paul told us clearly why we are motivated to live the sanctified lives we do, "For Christ's love compels us..." (2 Corinthians 5:14). And Jesus himself assures us, "As the Father has loved me, so have I loved you," (John 15:9).

Instead of living in a paranoid world wondering if roller skates are allowed, if their window sash has four or six panes of glass, if their hat brim is a half inch too narrow, if they are allowed to enjoy the sound of a violin, if their telephone is too close to their front door, if they are coveting by wanting air in their tractor tires, where they should part their hair, or if they want to speak English around the supper table, the Amish would do well to live their lives as a response to God's love instead of trying to earn God's love. Do their children ever get to sing the words "Jesus loves me, this I know?" Do their young folk ever realize that after they confess their sins there is a loving Shepherd waiting to take them into his arms once again? Do their old folk feel the glow of love that flows from the words of Psalm 23? Do they realize that for God, love is not a secondary afterthought but it is the driving force behind the suffering and death of Jesus Christ?

Sharing with the Amish

Sharing one's faith with the Amish is perhaps even more difficult than understanding their ways. To begin, not everyone lives near an Amish settlement. These districts are never just down the street, or in the apartment building next door. The Amish intentionally seek to live in places that are removed from society. The Plain People live in extremely closed societies. While there are exceptions, in general they do not welcome visitors. They do not want to learn more about you. They do not want to know who you are or what you believe. They do not want to sit down with you and tell you about their religion or to hear you tell them about yours. Rather they are taught to stay away from any close fellowship with the world. They cannot be seen or heard discussing religion with an outsider. That could mean immediate removal from their family and friends.

Consequently, sharing the love of Jesus with these people is a challenge of great proportion. However, that is not to say it is impossible. There are many within the Amish community who do realize that all is not well with their relationship with the Lord. There are those who are starved for the assurance of salvation, and who long to be held in the loving arms of their Savior, Jesus Christ, and to hear the assuring words that they have a place in heaven. I have heard of a van driver who transported Amish workmen to building sites and was able to share the love of God with some of those who rode with him. Their private discussions gave these Amish a hope they had never had. There are also organizations that make special efforts to distribute literature of hope and salvation within the Amish community. Amish responses range from total rejection and a "leave us alone" attitude, to "thank you, please send us some more information."

The worst we can do is to reject them because of their lifestyle, despise them and persecute them for their weakness of doctrine, or ignore them because they are too difficult to reach. We must never lose sight of the fact that these are struggling Christians who read from the same pages of Scripture as we. They are first cousins who have strayed into a confusing life that is sometimes just as puzzling to them as to us. We should pray that they would see the beautiful message of God's love and the assurance of salvation that is so clearly laid out in God's Word.

A puzzle indeed! Perhaps through a better understanding of what lies behind the ways and traditions of the Plain People can we better understand why they live as they do. Someone once said that these "are a people tied to the past but living in the present." The glue that holds their society together from generation to generation is their submission to the will of God as they understand it. They firmly believe that as long as they can remain focused on God's rules and promises, they will survive until he comes to take them home and give them an eternal rest far away from an ungodly world.

We have driven the back roads and discovered a hidden society of deeply religious people. At first glance, they appeared interesting and unique, definitely not our "normal" 21st century citizens. Yet the more we uncovered about their personal lives, their family lives, and their church lives, the more we noticed they are a people who have followed a wayward theology that has been holding them hostage for centuries. Our prayer should be that someday the Lord will cut through their written and unwritten rules and regulations, and let them discover the beauty, comfort, hope, freedom, and assurance that can be found only in the true gospel of Jesus Christ.

1. Ruth Irene Garrett, *Crossing Over*, p. 18.
2. Ibid, p. 19.

BIBLIOGRAPHY

Arthur, Anthony. *The Tailor-King*, New York: St. Martin's Press, 1999.

Dyck, Cornelius J. An *Introduction to Mennonite History*, Scottdale, Pennsylvania: Herald Press, 1993.

Eastern Pennsylvania Mennonite Church. *The Swiss Anabaptists*, 3rd ed. Ephata, Pennsylvania: Eastern Mennonite Publications, 1999.

Estep, William R. *The Anabaptist Story*, Grand Rapids: William B. Eerdmans Publishing Company, 1996.

Fisher, Sara E. and Rachel K. Stahl, *The Amish School*, Intercourse, Pennsylvania: Good Books, 1986.

Horst, Isaac R. *A Separate People*, Scottdale, Pennsylvania: Herald Press, 2000.

Igou, Brad, ed. *The Amish in Their Own Words*, Scottdale, Pennsylvania: Herald Press, 1999.

Garrett, Ruth Irene and Rick Farrant. *Crossing Over*, San Francisco, California: Harper Collins, 2003.

Garrett, Ruth Irene and Deborah Morse-Kahn. *Born Amish*, Paducah, Kentucky: Turner Publishing Company, 2004.

Good, Merle and Phyllis. *20 Most Asked Questions about the Amish and Mennonites*, Intercourse, Pennsylvania: Good Books, 1995.

Good, Phyllis Pellman and Jerry Irwin, *Amish Children*, Intercourse, Pennsylvania: Good Books, 2000.

Hostetler, John A. *Amish Society*, 4th ed., Baltimore: The Johns Hopkins University Press, 1993

_____. *The Amish*, Revised ed., Scottdale, Pennsylvania: Herald Press, 1995.

_____. *Hutterite Life*, Scottdale, Pennsylvania: Herald Press, 1983.

_____. *Amish Life*, Scottdale, Pennsylvania: Herald Press, 1983.

King, Christian E. and Isaac Stoltzfus. *Hymn Translations German to English from Ausbund and Lieder Buch*, Canada, 2000.

Klaassen, Walter. *Anabaptism: Neither Catholic nor Protestant*, 3rd ed. Kitchener, Ontario: Pandora Press, 2001.

Kraybill, Donald B. *The Riddle of Amish Culture*, Baltimore: The Johns Hopkins University Press, 2001.

_____. *Who Are the Anabaptists,* Scottdale, Pennsylvania: Herald Press, 2003.

Kraybill, Donald B. and Carl Desportes Bowman. *On the Backroad to Heaven,* Baltimore: The Johns Hopkins University Press, 2000.

Kraybill, Donald B. and C. Nelson Hostetter. *Anabaptist World USA,* Herald Press: Scottdale, Pennsylvania, 2001.

Kroeker, Wally, *An Introduction to the Russian Mennonites,* Intercourse, Pennsylvania: Good Books, 2005.

Loewen, Harry. *No Permanent City,* Scottdale, Pennsylvania: Herald Press, 1993.

Mead, Frank S., Samuel S. Hill and Craig D. Atwood, *Handbook of Denominations in the United States,* 12th ed., Nashville: Abingdon Press, 2005.

Miller, Mary M. *Our Heritage, Hope, and Faith,* ed. Walnut Creek: Carlisle Press. 2000.

Nolt, Steven M. *A History of the Amish,* Intercourse, Pennsylvania: Good Books, 1992.

Oyer, John S. and Robert S. Kreider, *Mirror of the Martyrs,* Intercourse, Pennsylvania: Good Books, 2003.

Scott, Stephen. *Amish Houses and Barns.* Intercourse, Pennsylvania: Good Books, 2001.

_____. *Plain Buggies,* Intercourse, Pennsylvania: Good Books, 1998.

Stoll, Joseph, *Fire in the Zurich Hills,* Aylmer, Ontario: Pathway Publishing Corporation, 1972 (reprint 1999.)

Van Bright, Thieleman J. ed. *Martyrs Mirror,* 25th ed., Scottdale, Pennsylvania: Herald Press, 2004.

Wenger, J. C. *What Mennonites Believe,* Scottdale, Pennsylvania: Herald Press, 1991.

Whittmer, Joe. The *Gentle People: Personal Reflections of Amish Life,* expanded ed., Minneapolis: Educational Media Corporation, 2001.

BIBLE CLASS STUDY AVAILABLE FROM AUTHOR REYNOLD R. KREMER

"The Plain People...Anabaptists: Hutterites, Mennonites, and the Amish"

This six session Bible class course prepared by Reynold R. Kremer is ideal for church groups or home Bible study classes. The course comes on a printable (reproducible) CD-Rom. Also available with this curriculum are two recommended videos: *"The Amish: A People of Preservation"*, and *"Hutterites"*. To order, or for additional information, call 1-800-669-0887.

Kremer Publications, Inc.
12615 W. Custer Avenue
Butler, WI 53007
www.kremerpublications.com